KIDS'
BIG
QUESTIONS
ABOUT
HEAVEN,
THE BIBLE,
AND OTHER REALLY IMPORTANT STUFF

Other Books by Sandy Silverthorne

Kids' BIG QUESTIONS ABOUT HEAVEN, THE BIBLE,

AND OTHER REALLY IMPORTANT STUFF

101 THINGS YOU WANT TO KNOW

SANDY SILVERTHORNE

Revell

a division of Baker Publishing Group
Grand Rapids, Michigan

Published by Revell
a division of Baker Publishing Group
Grand Rapids, Michigan
RevellBooks.com

Printed in the United States of America

Library of Congress Cataloging-in-Publication Data
Names: Silverthorne, Sandy, 1951- author.
Title: Kids' big questions about heaven, the Bible, and other really important stuff : 101 things you want to know / Sandy Silverthorne.
Description: Grand Rapids, Michigan : Revell, a division of Baker Publishing Group, [2024] | Audience: Ages 6–8 | Audience: Grades 2–3
Identifiers: LCCN 2023033404 | ISBN 9780800745431 (paper) | ISBN 9780800745714 (casebound) | ISBN 9781493444847 (ebook)
Subjects: LCSH: Christian children—Religious life—Juvenile literature. | Christian life—Juvenile literature. | Bible—Miscellanea—Juvenile literature. | Heaven—Juvenile literature. | Bible stories—Juvenile literature.
Classification: LCC BV4571.3 .S549 2024 | DDC 242/.62—dc23/eng/20230912
LC record available at https://lccn.loc.gov/2023033404

The author is represented by WordServe Literary Group, www.wordserveliterary.com.

Baker Publishing Group publications use paper produced from sustainable forestry practices and post-consumer waste whenever possible.

24 25 26 27 28 29 30   7 6 5 4 3 2 1

To Vicki—thanks for all the love, laughter,
and support you continue to give me.
I love exploring the BIG questions with you.

To Christy—you are such an awesome person
and a gift to so many. I love your humor,
creativity, and wisdom.

To the kids and leaders at Camp Harlow
in Eugene, Oregon—you inspire me with all of your
BIG questions about God, the Bible, and heaven.
For me, being at Harlow is like heaven on earth.

Contents

Contents

Contents

Contents

Contents

Contents

Introduction

What's heaven like? Are there angels there? Is it even *real* in the first place? Who wrote the Bible? Does God always answer our prayers? These and tons of other questions kids want to know about are all answered in this amazing and interesting book. Does God live in heaven? What will we do there? Will there be pizza?

There are some really cool and stunning things that God wants us to know. Like the fact that He created everything—the universe, the Pacific Ocean, Colorado, Japan, you, and me! He's watching us all the time, and He cares about every little detail of our lives—what foods we like, what games we like to play, and who our best friend is.

But there are other things about God, heaven, and the world that we don't know. These are things that are too big, mysterious, and wonderful for us to fully understand. After all, God is . . . well, God.

Check out Deuteronomy 29:29: "There are some things the Lord our God has kept secret. But there are some things he has let us know. These things belong to us and our children forever. It is so we will do everything in these teachings."

So even though there will be some things we don't understand right now, God loves when we search for answers. And that's what this book is all about. Finding out some amazing things about God, heaven, and some of God's incredible people.

So get ready to do some detective work and find out a whole lot of things about a whole lot of things.

What jobs won't we need in heaven? What will we do there?

Are there animals in heaven?

How did Gideon become so brave?

Why do we go to church?

Will we eat in heaven?

Did Jonah really get swallowed by a big fish?

What's heaven going to be like?

People will come from the east, west, north, and south.
They will sit down at the table in the kingdom of God.

Luke 13:29

Because we live on earth and it is all we've ever known, we might have a hard time imagining what heaven will be like. Also, books, TV shows, and movies often show heaven to be kind of unreal and cloudy, with people walking around slowly, looking kind of like angels, and everything is pretty quiet and peaceful. And while it will be a place of perfect peace, heaven won't be like what the movies tell us.

First of all, heaven won't be all misty and cloudy, filled with dry ice. It'll be solid, like the world we live in now. Actually, believe it or not, heaven is going to be even *more* solid than the world we live in now. The scenery is going to be incredible (think garden of Eden, only better). The hills will be greener, the water bluer and more sparkling, and the air sweet and pure. The colors of the trees and flowers will be more vivid, the food (yes, there will be food—more on that later) will taste better than anything you've ever tasted. And everyone who's there will be strong, healthy, and full of energy.

The Bible—we'll talk more about that later—says that God created heaven and that, yes, it is a real place. Some people would like to think that heaven is just a nice thought or a dream or an idea. But Jesus Himself talked about heaven being a real place. In fact, He even told His disciples that He was going there ahead of them to prepare a place for them (and that means for us too!). Cool, huh?

But the best thing of all about heaven is that God will be there. And if you want to know a secret, you can get a *tiny* glimpse of heaven in your life right now. How? By getting to know God for yourself. It's easier than you think. We'll talk more about how to do that in the coming chapters.

Is heaven a real place?

Our help comes from the Lord, who made heaven and earth.

Psalm 124:8

A lot of people think that heaven is a made-up place. I mean, it does sound almost too good to be true, right? But you know who thought heaven was real and not just pretend or imaginary? Jesus, that's who. And don't you think He should know? I mean, before He came to earth, that's where Jesus lived all the time! So He knew more than anybody how amazing and wonderful and awesome heaven is!

Jesus never said that heaven was just an idea or something in our minds. He always talked about heaven like it was real. Check out John 14:2–3:

There are many rooms in my Father's house. I would not tell you this if it were not true. I am going there to prepare a place for you. After I go and prepare a place for you, I will come back. Then I will take you to be with me so that you may be where I am.

19

This is the only place in the whole New Testament where Jesus says, "I would not tell you this if it were not true." He wanted us to know for sure that heaven is a real place.

Even though heaven is hard to completely understand and we can't see it (at least not yet!), it is a real place, and as we continue to follow Jesus, someday we'll meet Him there, right in the middle of it!

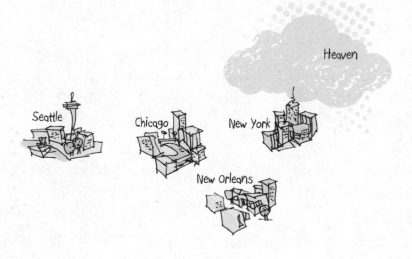

Heaven Is a Real Place

All throughout this book we'll have some "Talk It Over" sections where you can discuss what you've been reading with your mom, dad, or small group. Feel free to discuss the topics that don't have these sections too! But now, take a few minutes to talk about this chapter and what you've learned. Remember there are no wrong answers, just a chance to dig deeper into what you've been reading.

When we talk about heaven, it almost sounds too good to be true, doesn't it? No more pain or sickness or sadness, and everybody is going to get along! It sounds like a fairy-tale, happily-ever-after ending. Can it really be true? Is it a real place?

1. Think of some reasons we can believe that heaven is real and not a made-up idea just to make us feel better. (Hint: Jesus talked a lot about heaven. And there are other places in the Bible where it's referred to as a real place. Here are some of them: John 14:2; 1 Cor. 2:9; Phil. 3:20; 2 Tim. 4:18.)

2. Can you find some places in your Bible where Jesus talks about heaven?

3. If heaven is real and God wants us to live there forever, how can that make a difference in how we live now? Or does it?

4. If you were God, what are some things you would make sure were in heaven?

Close by spending some time in prayer for one another. Share with others some needs that you have and let them pray for you.

What will I look like in heaven?

Look at my hands and my feet. It is I myself! Touch me. You can see that I have a living body; a ghost does not have a body like this.

Luke 24:39

Sometimes if you see a TV show or movie about heaven, the people there are kind of semi-invisible, or ghostlike. They sometimes float around and usually live in clouds and fog. But that's not the way it's going to be. You'll look just like you do now, only with a new body that will never hurt, get sick, or struggle. How do we know that?

After Jesus died and rose again (yeah, He really did that—more on that later), He wasn't see-through or like a ghost or spirit. He looked just like He had before, only now He was alive again! All of His friends recognized Him, talked to Him, and even ate some fish and bread with Him. And He even told one of them, Thomas, to touch Him and see that He was real!

So from this we can figure out that when we get to heaven, we'll have real bodies too. Actual, for-real arms and legs and a head and feet and everything we have now. Only MUCH better!

Will I recognize my family and friends?

The follower whom Jesus loved said to Peter, "It is the Lord!"

John 21:7

This is like question 3, "What will I look like in heaven?" Of course, you'll recognize your family—they'll look just the way they do now, only maybe a different age. And just like Jesus's friends knew Him after He rose from the dead, you'll recognize people, and they'll recognize you too! When He was here on earth, Jesus mentioned that our family relationships will be a little different—check it out in Matthew 22:30:

When people rise from death, there will be no marriage. People will not be married to each other. They will be like the angels in heaven.

But remember this: We'll still know one another and be closer than we ever were before.

Draw a picture of your family. Don't forget your pets!

Do I have to be good to go to heaven?

As the Scriptures say: "There is no one without sin. None!"

Romans 3:10

This is probably the BIGGEST question that kids (and adults!) have about getting to heaven. After all, aren't you just supposed to be good, at least good enough for God to welcome you into heaven? But the truth of the matter is—get ready—NOBODY is good enough to get to heaven! *What? That doesn't sound too good!*

Let's put it this way: Have you ever done or said or even *thought* anything that was bad? Maybe you hit your little brother or talked back to a teacher or even thought about doing something mean to someone else. Then you're just like every person who's ever lived. Not perfect. And unfortunately the bad stuff we do keeps us separate from God and even heaven. Arrgghh! You might be saying, "I don't want to hear that!"

The truth is, there's only one person who ever lived a perfect enough life to get to heaven, and that was Jesus.

And guess what? He didn't want to go there without us! So God came up with an amazing plan to take care of our separation problem and make it possible for all of us to join Him in heaven forever! You'll learn about what that plan was in question 90.

Never Good Enough

It's not good news when you hear that none of us is ever going to be good enough to get to heaven. But God knew we couldn't! Discuss the following questions and talk about what God might do to help us come back to Him.

1. Can you think of a time when you did something really nice for someone without being asked?

2. Talk about a time when you were disobedient to your parents, a teacher, or a friend. How did it feel?

3. What do you think of the idea that none of us is good enough to go to heaven? (Check out Rom. 3:10.)

4. If you were God, how would you make it possible for people to go to heaven?

5. Did you know that God *did* make a way for all of us to live with Him forever in heaven? Jesus did it by taking our place and our *punishment* for the bad stuff we do. Talk a little about that.

Spend a couple minutes sharing some things you'd like to pray about, then pray for one another.

Will there be girls in heaven?

(Asked by an eight-year-old boy)

> So God created human beings in his image. In the image of God he created them. He created them male and female.
>
> Genesis 1:27

This question was actually asked of me at a summer camp for third through fifth graders. Apparently, this particular lad was having trouble with either a neighbor or, more than likely, a sister, and the thought of having to spend eternity with this girl was just too much for him to bear. So I felt bad having to tell him that, yes, there will most certainly be girls in heaven.

In fact, the apostle Paul talked about this when he told the people of Galatia that when we begin to follow Jesus, there's no difference between Jews and non-Jews, workers and bosses, or, yes, even men and women! Since the beginning of time, God has loved everyone—boys, girls, men, women, adults, little kids, and old people.

And the best news yet? He loves *you*!

So will there be girls in heaven? Absolutely! And since we know that heaven's going to be wonderful and there will be no more trouble, hurt feelings, or arguments, we can be sure that we'll all get along perfectly. Boys *and* girls.

Who was Noah? Did he really build a big boat?

[Noah] and his wife and his sons and their wives went into the boat. They went in to escape the waters of the flood.

Genesis 7:7

At the time when Noah was around, thousands of years before Jesus, the world was a crazy, scary place. People weren't following God; they were killing, fighting, robbing, and hurting one another. Things got so bad that even God was sorry He'd created people.

But . . .

There was one guy who loved God and obeyed Him in everything he did. His name was Noah. So God told him to build a big boat and then collect his family and two of every kind of animal and get them into the boat (or ark, as they called it). This way they'd be safe when God flooded the earth and wiped out every living thing. So even though this whole thing was pretty hard to believe—a worldwide flood?—Noah obeyed God and built the ark. It had to be huge! It was about 450 feet long, 75 feet wide, and 45 feet high, and some believe it could have held as many as 330 railroad cars. So at God's instructions, Noah gathered his wife, three sons, and their wives, and they joined all the animals in the ark. Then it started to rain. And rain. And rain. God also released huge fountains of water from underground that created gigantic waves that soon covered the entire earth. After a while, the water reached up to the very tops of the mountains! And all the living things on earth were wiped out.

Noah and his family must have been pretty busy for a long time taking care of all the lions, tigers, koala bears, cats, monkeys, dogs, parrots, wolves (you get the idea)

inside the ark. After a long time, the flood waters started to go down and the ark rested on a tall mountain called Mount Ararat. Then Noah, his family, and all the animals came out and started life all over again. They'd been protected and they got a brand-new start because Noah obeyed God.

Can you imagine all those animals on the ark? Think about some of your favorite animals. Make a list of or draw some of your favorites and what they might have looked like while riding on Noah's big boat.

DID YOU KNOW?

Here's a little quiz from the Old Testament:

How long was Noah inside the ark during the great flood?

  A. Two months
  B. Over a year
  C. Forty days and forty nights

If you guessed B, you are right! Although the Bible says that God made it *rain* for forty days and forty nights, it was over a year before Noah and his family came out of the ark!

Check out Genesis 7 and 8, and add up the days they spent in Noah's big boat.

Will there be animals in heaven?

Calves, lions and young bulls will eat together.
And a little child will lead them.

Isaiah 11:6

Lots of people, especially kids, want to know the answer to this question. Will there be cats, dogs, horses, and even koala bears in heaven? Since people and animals are different—people are made in God's image, so we're really special to God—we don't know for sure if there will be animals in heaven, but we can guess that there will be for two reasons.

One is that when God created the world (and the entire universe, for that matter), one of the first things He made were animals. He created this perfect place, the garden of Eden, and filled it with tigers, ostriches, porcupines, and iguanas. And a whole lot of other animals! And since the garden of Eden was perfect, all the animals—and even the people—got along in perfect peace. Since heaven is going to be perfect, it seems like God will have lots of animals up there too.

Think of it this way: If animals give us great joy and happiness here on earth, I'll bet God will give them to us in heaven.

Number two: There's a Scripture in the Old Testament book of Isaiah that most people think describes the new world that Jesus will bring about when He comes again. And look carefully. You might find a clue about animals in the passage!

> So a new king will come
>> from the family of Jesse. [That's Jesus!] . . .
> Then wolves will live in peace with lambs.
>> And leopards will lie down to rest with goats.
> Calves, lions and young bulls will eat together.
>> And a little child will lead them.

Cows and bears will eat together in peace.
   Their young will lie down together.
   Lions will eat hay as oxen do. (11:1, 6–7)

Wow! Wolves, lambs, leopards, goats, cows, lions, and bears! This might just be a clue that, yes indeed, there might really be animals in heaven.

Do you have a pet? Or more than one? Draw a picture of your pet or favorite animal.

Will I be an angel in heaven?

> Praise him, all you angels.
> Praise him, all you armies of heaven.
>
> Psalm 148:2

Lots of times when people think about heaven, they assume that the angels up there are people who have died. After all, doesn't the Bible say that people go to heaven after this life? And doesn't it also say that there are tons of angels in heaven? Right on both counts. But people don't become angels when they die. Angels are a different kind of created being. They serve God by delivering messages for Him and even fighting battles,

but they were created to live in heaven and to serve that special purpose.

And even though angels will live forever, they haven't been around forever like God and Jesus. They were created, just like us. But people are different from angels. Angels have special jobs to do, and we do too.

And even though we won't become angels when we get to heaven, God created us for really special purposes. He made us to live on earth, to get to know Him, and to reflect His love wherever we go.

What's the deal with angels anyway?

> All the angels are spirits who serve God and are sent to help those who will receive salvation.
>
> Hebrews 1:14

People have been fascinated with angels since . . . well, forever. There are accounts in the Bible where people have encountered angels in all kinds of situations. Joshua saw an angel outside the city of Jericho who encouraged him before the battle (Josh. 5:13–15). Gideon, when he was hiding from his enemies, met an angel who called him a mighty warrior (Judg. 6:11–12). An angel told Mary she was going to be the mother of Jesus (Luke 1:26–33), and an angel told her husband, Joseph, to protect Mary and the baby Jesus by escaping to Egypt when King Herod tried to hunt them down (Matt. 2:13–18).

Angels are heavenly beings who often appear as people in the Bible and usually have some kind of message for someone. An angel told a couple in Israel they were going to have a baby and to name him Samson. Angels appeared to the shepherds to announce and celebrate Jesus's birth, and at least one angel told the disciples that Jesus had risen from the dead.

Angels deliver messages, worship God, and even intervene in things going on here on earth. And even though angels are cool, they like to stay behind the scenes, so we don't ever have to worship or even talk to them.

We can always pray to God, and He'll take care of us, even if it means sending an angel to help.

We'll see plenty of angels in heaven, and believe it or not, they'll think we're pretty cool because we followed God here on earth even when we couldn't see Him. Here on earth, we need faith to believe, but in heaven, angels get to see God face-to-face all the time (Matt. 18:10).

By the Way: The Angel of the Lord

Several times in the Old Testament somebody gets face-to-face with someone called "the angel of the Lord." Most people who study this kind of thing believe this angel was actually Jesus before He came to earth as a man. Pretty cool, huh? Some of the people who met the angel of the Lord were Abraham (Gen. 18:1–3), Joshua (Josh. 5:13–15), Gideon (Judg. 6:11–12), and Samson's parents (Judg. 13).

Who were Jesus's disciples? How many were there?

The next morning, Jesus called his followers to him.
He chose 12 of them, whom he named "apostles."

Luke 6:13

This is kind of a trick question. When we think of Jesus's disciples, we usually think of the twelve guys whom He chose to hang out with Him most of the time. Their names were Simon Peter, his brother Andrew, James and his brother John, Philip, Bartholomew, Thomas, Matthew, another James, Thaddaeus, Simon the Zealot, and Judas Iscariot, the one who betrayed Jesus.

And these guys were an interesting bunch. Peter, James, and John were fishermen, and Thomas had some doubts about some of the things Jesus did. Simon hated the Romans who governed the Jewish people at that time, yet he was a disciple alongside Matthew, who collected taxes for the Romans! Wonder how those two got along.

In Luke 10:1 Jesus sends out seventy-two people to spread the good news about Him to others. So at that point we know there were at least seventy-two disciples. And in Acts 2:41, the number of disciples grows from 120 to over 3,000 in one day! So even though we think of the twelve when we hear about His disciples, there were a lot more.

So what makes a person a disciple?

First of all, the word *disciple* sounds a little like the word *discipline*, and it just means someone who's studying something or someone. And a lot of the people we read about in the New Testament followed, studied, and wanted to become like Jesus. Not just the twelve but many more.

And the best news of all? If you're following Jesus, reading your Bible, and talking to Him through prayer, you're one of His disciples too!

Who were Adam and Eve? Were they really the first people on earth?

The man gave names to all the tame animals, to the birds in the sky and to all the wild animals. But Adam did not find a helper that was right for him.

Genesis 2:20

The man named his wife Eve. This is because she is the mother of everyone who ever lived.

Genesis 3:20

At the beginning of the Bible, in Genesis 2, we learn about Adam and Eve, the first man and woman in creation. After God created the heavens and the earth, the oceans, the land, and all the animals, He created a man. God called him Adam, or "man." One of Adam's first jobs was to name all the animals God had created. But even though all the animals—the lions, bears, dolphins, kangaroos, and lizards—were there with Adam, God still noticed that Adam needed a partner. So He created the first woman—Eve.

Adam and Eve lived in an incredible place called the garden of Eden, which was located where Iraq is today. Even though the garden doesn't still exist, a couple rivers that bordered it—the Tigris and the Euphrates—do. So Adam and Eve lived in this wonderful paradise and had a perfect life living at peace with each other and all the animals.

God told Adam and Eve that they could eat the fruit from any of the trees in the garden except one—the fruit that would give them the knowledge of good and evil.

After a while, Eve was fooled by a snake (it was actually the devil), who told her to disobey God and go ahead and eat that forbidden fruit. So she and Adam ate the fruit God had told them not to eat. After that, their friendship with God was broken. Even though He still loved them, they had to leave the garden. Soon, sickness, disease, pain, and fear were introduced for the first time on the planet, and the world wasn't perfect anymore.

Who was Gideon? How did he become so brave?

The angel of the Lord appeared to Gideon and said, "The Lord is with you, mighty warrior!"

Judges 6:12

The story of Gideon in the book of Judges in the Old Testament is a great one! When an angel showed up to meet Gideon, Gideon was hiding out from a bunch of bullies called the Midianites. They'd stormed into Israel and ruined all the crops that God's people had grown for the entire year! When the angel greeted Gideon and told him he was going to defeat the Midianites, Gideon couldn't believe it. But slowly, day by day, Gideon learned to trust God and obey what He said.

But Gideon still needed some assurance. So he put a fleece (wool from a lamb) out during the night and told God, "If the fleece is wet in the morning and the ground is dry, then I'll believe You're in this and leading me." Well, the next morning that's exactly what happened. The fleece was damp and the ground was dry. But Gideon still wasn't convinced. "Okay, Lord," he said, "this time let's see if the fleece will be dry and the ground wet; then I'll believe Your plan for me." God didn't even get upset with Gideon's request. So sure enough, that's what happened the next day.

Fleece dry.

Ground wet.

So Gideon took his men—three hundred of them—and surrounded the camp of the Midianites late at night. Gideon's men blew their horns and held up their torches, and the Midianites panicked. They started fighting each other! Gideon's army hardly had to do anything because God was the one who was fighting the battle.

Gideon is a great example of what can happen when we trust God and do what He says.

What jobs won't we need in heaven?

Part 1

May the favor of the Lord our God rest on us;
  establish the work of our hands for us—
  yes, establish the work of our hands.

Psalm 90:17 NIV

You might not have ever thought about this question, but it's a fun one to consider. After all, things are going to be perfect in heaven, so there will be no more need for:

1. Undertakers—These are the people who take care of people after they die. Since nobody's ever going to die in heaven—no undertakers.
2. Doctors—Nobody will ever get sick or hurt up there, so there will be no need for doctors or nurses.

3. Dentists—You won't have any cavities, and apparently your teeth will be perfect, so no more trips to the dentist. Or the orthodontist.

4. Soldiers—We won't have any wars or invasions in heaven, so there will be no more need for soldiers, sailors, or even the Air Force. Hope we still have planes though.

5. Police officers—There will be no more crime, so no laws will be broken or even need to be enforced. So no police officers will be necessary.

6. Prison guards—No prisons in heaven, so there won't be any need for guards, wardens, prison cooks, or prison laundry workers.

There are a few more ideas of what jobs we won't need in heaven on the next page.

15

What jobs won't we need in heaven?

Part 2

In all the work you are doing, work the best you can.
Work as if you were working for the Lord, not for men.

Colossians 3:23

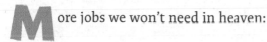

More jobs we won't need in heaven:

1. Optometrists—These are the people who check your vision, prescribe glasses, and help you see better. Since all of our bodies will be perfect in heaven, our vision will be 20/20 too. We'll be able to see perfectly.

2. Lifeguards—Lifeguards are those men and women who protect us when we're swimming in the ocean, at a lake, or in the pool. But since we'll all be able to swim just great, no need for lifeguards!

3. Insurance salespeople—People buy insurance to pay money to cover expenses after accidents or

when someone dies. But in heaven? No accidents and nobody ever dies. No need for insurance!

4. Fitness and beauty businesspeople—Once again, we'll have perfect, healthy bodies, and everyone will reflect Jesus in all they do, so we won't need to train or have beauty treatments.

5. Auto-repair workers—I'm not sure if there will be cars in heaven, but if there are, since there won't be any accidents, no need for repairs!

So what will all these people be doing in heaven if their jobs won't exist? Good question. Everybody's going to work in heaven as they serve God, whether they were a waitress, surgeon, painter, or plumber here in this world. In heaven, we may not do the jobs we did here on earth, but since things will be amazing and perfect up there, you can be sure that our work's going to be perfectly designed for us.

List some other jobs you think won't be in heaven.

16

Why is it important for us to worship God?

Let everything that breathes praise the Lord. Praise the Lord!

Psalm 150:6

You may have heard that we'll all be worshiping God a lot when we get to heaven. Why is that so important? In fact, why is it important for us to worship Him now? Well, when you think about it, He's the biggest, grandest, greatest person in the whole universe! He created the heavens and the earth, the stars, the sun, the moon, and every single person who ever lived! He's smart enough to figure out how to run the world and close enough to understand all our thoughts, fears, dreams, and feelings. So in other words, He's totally worth worshiping!

There are lots of ways to worship God. If you go to a church, Sunday school, or youth group, you might sing songs that praise God during the meeting. By the way, you can always sing to God at home in your room or out in your backyard by yourself too.

Another way to worship God is to thank Him for all the cool things He's done for you.

Tell Him thanks for your family, today's breakfast, your dog or cat, and maybe even your teacher and the friends in your class or neighborhood.

One of the best reasons it's good to worship God is because it reminds you how BIG He is and how small you are. He's big enough to handle anything you might face, and He cares about every part of your life.

He knows you and loves you. 'Cause you're His kid!

17

Will I see God when I get to heaven?

Happy are those whose hearts are pure, for they shall see God.

Matthew 5:8 TLB

Since God is Spirit, nobody's really seen what He looks like. There are a couple guys in the Old Testament portion of the Bible who got a glimpse of God. One was a guy named Isaiah. He saw God in heaven sitting on a throne (Isa. 6:1). That must have been an incredible experience! Also, Moses got the chance to see the back of God passing by in Exodus 33:19–23.

But when we get to heaven, the Bible says God will be close enough to wipe away a tear from your eye. How cool is that? But for now, the best way to see God is to read and learn a lot about Jesus. For not only was Jesus a great man who healed people, taught all kinds of cool stuff, and even walked on water, but He was God in person form! So whenever you look at Jesus, you're really looking at God!

Read all about Him in the book of Matthew, Mark, Luke, or John in the New Testament.

Every time we read about Jesus, we can discover new things about God the Father. And yes, when you get to heaven you will be able to see God in person and face-to-face!

What happens when you die? Do you go straight to heaven?

> Then Jesus said to him, "Listen! What I say is true: Today you will be with me in paradise!"
>
> Luke 23:43

This is a great question and one people have been wondering about for two thousand years. But when we look in the Bible, it sure appears that we go straight to heaven to see Jesus the moment we stop living here on earth.

Here are a couple reasons to think that:

1. When Jesus was hanging on the cross, there were two guys hanging on crosses next to Him who had been robbers. One of them was mad at everybody, even Jesus. But the other one knew that he deserved to be punished (not that anyone deserves to be hung on a cross). He also knew that Jesus had never done anything wrong. He called

to Jesus and asked Him to remember him when Jesus went into His kingdom, and Jesus said to him, "Listen! What I say is true: *Today* you will be with me in paradise!" (emphasis added).

Wow, today! That means this guy was going to be with Jesus in heaven right away. And live with Him forever!

2. Another verse in the New Testament was written by one of Jesus's followers named Paul. In 2 Corinthians 5:6–8, he writes that to be absent from the body is to be present with the Lord. He was convinced that when we die, we are immediately in the presence of Jesus.

That's pretty cool, huh? So what do we do in the meantime? Well, try this—get to know Jesus by reading your Bible, talking to Him in prayer, serving people, and hanging out with other Jesus followers. That way you'll grow in your faith and learn to be a blessing to others.

How old will I be in heaven?

You are young, but do not let anyone treat you as if you were not important. Be an example to show the believers how they should live. Show them with your words, with the way you live, with your love, with your faith, and with your pure life.

1 Timothy 4:12

The Bible never tells us how old we'll be in heaven, but there are a couple theories floating around that are fun to think about. The most popular theories are that all of us will be around thirty or thirty-three years old when we're in heaven.

This is because of two reasons: One is that, humanly speaking, people are at their peak physically and mentally around thirty years old. When you're younger than that, you're still growing, and when you're a lot older than that, depending on how you take care of yourself, things in your body might not work so well. So since heaven is going to be perfect, a lot of people figure we'll be around thirty years old once we get there.

The other reason people tend to think we'll be that age in heaven is that Jesus started His ministry at age thirty. And since the Bible says we're going to be like Him forever, it might mean we'll be about the age He was when He died, rose, and went to heaven. Which would be thirty-three years old.

All that may be true, or we all may be way off on the whole heaven-age thing, but you can be sure God is going to do the perfect thing for us. Whatever age we're going to be in heaven, God's going to make it—and us—perfect!

Who was Jonah? Did he really get swallowed by a fish?

> Jesus answered, . . . "Jonah was in the stomach of the big fish for three days and three nights."
>
> Matthew 12:39–40

There's an account in the Old Testament about a guy named Jonah, and it's a great story full of storms, plants, worms, frightened sailors, and yes, a big man-swallowing fish.

It seems that God wanted Jonah as one of His spokesmen to go to this awful city named Nineveh and tell these people about how much God loved them.

Well, Jonah knew two things:

1. The people who lived in Nineveh were terrible. They were violent and bloodthirsty and they hated everyone.

2. And Jonah also knew that God *loved* everyone, even the people of Nineveh, and he knew that

God would forgive them and save them from disaster, and Jonah didn't want that to happen.

So he ran away from God (like that's possible), got on a ship headed in the opposite direction from Nineveh, and went down to the lower deck and fell asleep.

Well, God didn't give up on Jonah. He sent a storm to slow down the ship. It got so bad that the sailors thought the ship was going to sink and that they'd all die. Jonah came up and told them the storm was his fault and asked them to throw him overboard (I told you this was a great story), so they did.

But just as Jonah was about to sink, God sent a big fish to swallow him whole. Whew.

So Jonah stayed in the belly of the fish (stinky!) until he finally prayed to God. Then God told the fish to throw up Jonah on the shore.

At last, Jonah got the message, went to Nineveh, and told them about God. They listened, turned from their wicked ways, and God saved them, just like Jonah knew He would.

If you want to read more about the worm and the plant I mentioned earlier, read the book of Jonah in the Old Testament.

Is it possible that a man could survive being inside a fish? Yeah. Well, think about it: God can do anything He wants, so if He wanted Jonah to be in the fish for a few days, or a couple years, He could do it.

What is the most important thing for us to do to follow God?

The Pharisee asked, "Teacher, which command in the law is the most important?"

Matthew 22:36

A man asked Jesus this very question in Matthew 22:36. He asked what the most important commandment was for people to follow. Jesus answered by saying that we need to love God with all our heart, our thoughts, and our strength. And then He said to love our neighbor as ourselves. That one can be pretty hard. We all need God's help to care for someone as much as we care about ourselves. So Jesus basically said if you want to please God, love Him and love people. Pretty simple, huh?

This doesn't mean that you have to earn God's love by working at it. God loves you, has loved you, and will love you for all eternity. And His number one priority is a friendship with you. But once you begin a friendship with God through Jesus, you'll start to grow in your love for God and for other people. It's a natural response to all the good things God does for you.

What are some ways you can show God how much you love Him?

What are some things you can do to show people around you that you love them?

Is there music in heaven?

> They were saying, "Amen! Praise, glory, wisdom, thanks, honor, power, and strength belong to our God forever and ever. Amen!"
>
> Revelation 7:12

The Bible, which is God's Word to us, tells us that the angels worship God all the time in heaven. And we will too. Only it'll be the most amazing, beautiful, full, alive music in the whole universe! And it will draw all of us in and surround us like a wonderful, warm, pure ocean wave.

Nowadays we've got all kinds of music around us, but since God is the most creative being in the universe (in fact, He created *creativity*!), the music we'll experience in heaven will be so much more fun, powerful, and beautiful than anything we've ever heard up to this point. It's like we'll actually live *inside* the music!

Experiencing the music of heaven compared to our music now will be like the difference between listening to the best, most famous orchestra in the entire world and listening to a guy playing a kazoo. Yes, we will hear music in heaven, and it'll be spectacular!

Do you play a musical instrument? What is it? Piano? Violin? Guitar? Drums?

Draw a picture of you playing your instrument. If you don't play one, draw an instrument you'd like to play.

Will I meet new people in heaven?

Let us think about each other and help each other to show love and do good deeds.

Hebrews 10:24

Heaven is going to be the most amazing place ever! There will be all kinds of new things to see and experience, new stuff to enjoy, and people to get to know. And since there will be millions of them, chances are there will probably be some you will not have already met.

And there will be people from every place you can think of. They'll be from all over the world! India, Pakistan, Brazil, Denmark, China, Arizona, and Bozeman, Montana.

And here's the even more amazing part: They'll be from every *century* in history. When you're in heaven, you'll probably meet people from the Old Testament like Moses, Joseph, and

Samson. And people like Jesus's friends Peter and John. And Ruth, Esther, and Mary, Jesus's mom. And folks from the 1800s and the Revolutionary War and the time William Shakespeare was around writing plays. People from the Dark Ages and the 1950s.

You'll also get to meet people who are just like you and people who are way different. But we'll all have one incredible thing in common: We all love God and that makes us a family!

Making Lots of New Friends

When we finally get to heaven, there are going to be a ton of new people to meet. Millions of them, in fact. But don't worry, you'll have all eternity to get to know them! Here are some questions regarding friendship that you can discuss with your family:

1. Who is one person you'd really like to meet in heaven? Remember they can be from any time period—ancient times, the medieval period, or maybe even the 1960s!

2. Are you one of those people who make friends easily, or do you like to take a little longer to get to know somebody?

3. Do you like lots and lots of friends or just one or two really good ones?

4. What are some things you can do to be a good friend to somebody this week?

Spend a few minutes sharing some things that need prayer right now. God loves it when we talk to Him and ask Him to be involved in every part of our lives.

**Amazing People
from the Bible
You Need to Meet**

Who was Joseph?
Why were his brothers
so mean to him?

You meant to hurt me. But God turned your evil into
good. It was to save the lives of many people. And it
is being done.

Genesis 50:20

There's a story in the book of Genesis in the Old Testament about a guy named Jacob who had twelve
sons. Wow, twelve! Think about it. That must have been
some dinner table. One of the younger sons was named
Joseph, and he was also his dad's favorite. You can imagine how that worked out for the family. (This is a different
Joseph from the guy who was married to Mary, Jesus's
mom). So one day Jacob sent Joseph to report on his
brothers and bring word back to him.

When the other boys spotted Joseph coming, they got
together and decided to get rid of him. At first, they
thought they'd kill him, but then one of them got the

idea to sell him as a slave and make some money at the same time.

So they sold Joseph to these traders who were on their way to Egypt. Then those guys sold him to a guy named Potiphar, who was a higher-up in the Egyptian government.

Well, Potiphar learned to trust Joseph and let him take care of his whole house. But then Potiphar's wife told some lies about Joseph, and he got thrown into prison.

Whoa, this is beginning to sound like a soap opera.

While Joseph was there, he made friends with a couple of guys who also had been arrested. They had these dreams, Joseph figured out what they meant, and long story short, he not only got out of prison but ended up being second-in-command for the entire country. Wow!

But regarding the question of why Joseph's brothers were so mean to him, there might be a couple reasons:

1. Their dad made it no secret that Joseph was his favorite. After a few years of hearing, "Joseph this and Joseph that," his brothers probably got pretty jealous of the guy. Have you ever been jealous of somebody? How did it feel?

2. Another reason these guys were upset with Joseph was because their dad even made him a fancy new coat of many colors, the kind a prince

might wear. None of the other brothers got one. This also probably made them mad. How would you feel if that happened to you?

Even keeping these things in mind, the brothers had no right to treat Joseph the way they did. But at the end of the story, Joseph ended up forgiving them and even helping them. For he saw that God had worked the whole thing out, not just for their benefit but for the benefit of the whole country. How cool is that?

Check out Joseph's amazing story in Genesis 37–50.

A Little Bible Quiz about Joseph

When Joseph's brothers' jealousy got the best of them, what did they do to Joseph?

- A. Ripped off his many-colored coat and tore it up.
- B. Threw him into a pit.
- C. Sold him as a slave to a passing caravan.
- D. All of the above.

If you chose D, "All of the above," you were right! Sounds pretty bad, but they took his coat and tore it to make it look like he'd been attacked by a wild animal. They threw him into a pit and were going to leave him there, until they saw the caravan and a chance to make some money. So they pulled him out and sold him as a slave to the traders. But God used all of this bad stuff to bless Joseph and even his brothers later on.

Where is heaven?

For as the heavens are high above the earth,
So great is His mercy toward those who fear Him.

Psalm 103:11 NKJV

Okay, get ready to have your head explode or at least your brain expand. Here goes—even though heaven is a real place, it's in another dimension, so we can't see it . . . yet.

The Bible talks about it being "up" because when Jesus died, rose from the dead, and then went to heaven, He went up. All His friends stood there looking up into the sky, so it sounds like He went up when He went to heaven.

But just because heaven is up, it doesn't mean you can see the place. Even if you took a rocket up into the upper stratosphere, you still wouldn't see heaven. Because it's not a visible place we can see right now.

There's a lot we don't know about heaven, but we can be sure of several things:

1. Even though we can't see it now, heaven is a real place. See question 2. It's more real than the world we know around us.

2. If we are followers of Jesus, either we'll see heaven someday when we die or God will reveal heaven to us when He comes back to set the world right. In fact, He promises that He's going to make a brand-new world with no wars or diseases or natural disasters or pain. At that point, it'll be like God will pull back the curtain so we can experience heaven.

3. The Bible talks about heaven a lot, but it never says where its location is. This is because heaven is where God is, and He'd like us to focus more on our friendship with Him than where heaven is located.

Up Above Us

The New Testament was originally written in the Greek language. The Greek word for heaven is *ouranos*, which means the sky and all the places above the earth. *Ouranos* also means the place where God lives. That's probably why we think of heaven as up above us.

26

Will we eat in heaven?

The kingdom of heaven is like a king who prepared a wedding feast for his son.

Matthew 22:2

It's kind of hard to imagine being somewhere for, like, forever and never having a meal. Since you were born, you've always eaten two, three, or maybe even four or five meals a day! So what happens in heaven? Are we going to eat up there? Where do we get the food? Who prepares it? Well, let's start off with the first question, Will we want to eat?

When you look at Jesus after He rose from the dead (and that's a pretty good way to figure out what *we'll* be like), you see that He ate a couple times with His friends.

In Luke 24:30, Jesus shared some bread with a couple guys He met along the road leading out of Jerusalem. And when He showed up to the disciples in a locked room, one of the first things He said was "Do you have anything to eat?" So they rustled up some bread and fish for Him.

Then later, while they were up on the beach by the Sea of Galilee, Jesus made a little campfire breakfast (again, with fish and bread) for His eleven disciples (John 21:12–14). So there's that.

Jesus told a story of how, when we're all together up in heaven with God, He's going to serve us a huge banquet. And it sounds like it'll be all you can eat! I'm not sure what they'll be serving, but I know it'll be amazing!

And since Jesus seemed to show up hungry after He rose again, it seems like we might eat on a regular basis when we're in heaven, and God will supply all the food we need!

What are some of your favorite foods? List them here or draw a picture of them. Don't forget the ice cream, toppings, and whipped cream!

27

I'm not a very good singer. Will I still be able to worship God in heaven?

Make a joyful noise unto the Lord.
Psalm 100:1 KJV

Remember, everything in heaven is going to be perfect! So your voice is going to be perfect too. Don't worry. You'll sound amazing! Besides, here are a couple things to think about:

1. When you stand before God in heaven, you'll be so taken with His power, majesty, and love, you'll forget all about what you sound like. Worship and praise, musical and not, will just come pouring out of your mouth. Think about the last time you were rooting for a team you loved. When they scored, whether it was a touchdown, goal, or home run, you probably started cheering—LOUD! You didn't even think about how you sounded. When you see God for the first time, it'll be so

much greater and more awesome than that, so you'll praise Him without even thinking about how you sound.

2. Here's a little secret: God doesn't care *how* your voice sounds. In fact, Psalm 100:1 says, "Make a joyful *noise* unto the Lord" (KJV, emphasis added). He doesn't care about the quality of our singing—even if it sounds a little, well . . . noisy. He just loves that we're telling Him how much we love Him.

And we'll get to do that a lot when we're in heaven.

28

Can we really talk to God? How do we do that?

People, trust God all the time.
Tell him all your problems.
God is our protection.

Psalm 62:8

Can you imagine if you could just pick up the phone and talk to the president? Or your favorite pro athlete or music star? That would be pretty amazing. But you want to know something even more amazing? You can talk to the One who created the universe and every living thing. Anytime you want. And you don't even need a phone!

God loves it when we talk to Him. (It's called praying.) In fact, He even encourages us to do it. And it's easier than you think.

You don't have to use special words when you pray or wait for a certain time of day. Just let Him know what's going on in your life. Thank Him for all the good stuff: a good grade on a quiz, going for pizza or burgers for dinner, meeting a new friend, or going on a trip.

And let Him know about the stuff that's hard for you too; He really wants to know. And He wants to help. Let Him know if you're nervous or scared about something. Or feeling lonely. Or if somebody was mean to you today. Anything that bothers you might just bother Him too. The important thing is to be honest with God.

And your prayer doesn't have to be fancy or sound grown-up. You might just say something like,

Dear God, thank You so much for being so awesome and thank You that You always have time to hear from me. Thank You for giving me time to play with my brother today, and thanks that we've been getting along better lately. Help me with my schoolwork and help me play well in my game this afternoon. Thanks a lot, amen.

See? Easy, right? Start praying today. It's one way to get closer to God.

Will there be enough room for everyone in heaven?

> I am going there to prepare a place for you.
>
> John 14:2

If there are eight billion people on earth right now (that's a lot!), and a lot of them love God, how is heaven going to fit them all? Not to mention all the Jesus followers who have lived before us. How is God going to make enough room for everyone to be in heaven? Won't it be crowded?

When we think of things in terms of what we know about earth, then it does seem like heaven is going to be really crowded. But we've got to remember that heaven isn't like earth. It's a completely new, different, and more wonderful place than we can even imagine.

And since God created heaven knowing we were going to be living there with Him forever, you know it's going to be perfect, comfortable, and if necessary, HUGE. Jesus told His disciples in John 14:2 that He was going to go and prepare a place for them (and US!) if they trusted

Him, loved Him, and followed Him. And Jesus doesn't lie. If He says He's going to make a place for us, we can count on it!

And if Jesus is going to prepare a place for us, then you can be sure it'll be amazing and there will be plenty of places and *space* for all of us. Remember God created the whole universe, so He'll make sure there will be plenty of space for all of us in heaven.

Will I still be my parents' kid in heaven?

Every family in heaven and on earth gets its true name from him.

Ephesians 3:15

When we talk about heaven, we begin to realize it's going to be a lot different than things are here on earth. We'll never get tired. We won't have arguments or misunderstandings with other people. It'll be beautiful and unlike anything we've ever experienced before. But the one thing that will be the same in heaven as it is here on earth is that we'll have relationships. In fact, one of the only things we'll be able to "take" to heaven with us is other people!

So if your parents (or cousins, siblings, or friends, for that matter) know Jesus and have decided to follow Him here on earth, then yes, you'll all be together in heaven.

And even though we'll have our forever bodies up there, we'll still recognize each family member, and we'll be closer with them than ever.

But there is one thing to remember. God tells us that we're *all* His kids and that we're all part of His big family first. And that makes the whole world our brothers and sisters!

Are there friends or family members you know who still don't know Jesus? Make a list of four or five of them and pray for them to come to know the Lord.

One Big Family

Families are an important part of helping us become who we are. We may not always get along with the people in our family, but God wants us to love them and respect them all the time. Even when it comes time to share our room!

1. What are some things you love about your family?

2. Are there some family traditions that you really like? Different things your family does together around Christmas, birthdays, or other holidays? Name a few of those favorite traditions.

3. Can you think of a funny memory you have with your family?

4. Who taught you how to ride a bike? Tie your shoes? Shoot a basket?

5. What's your favorite time of day? Morning? Breakfast with everybody? Dinner around the table? Bedtime?

Bonus: What is something you can do today to serve someone in your family?

Will I see people I know in heaven?

Perfume and oils make you happy.
And good advice from a friend is sweet.

Proverbs 27:9

Of course, you will! In fact, heaven's going to be the biggest family/friend/acquaintance reunion ever! Think about a wonderful family Christmas party you went to. Or a camping trip with your friends and family members. How about a birthday party where everyone you can think of was there? Well, heaven is going to be just like that, only a million times better! You'll see lots of your friends and people you know now, but also, as I mentioned in question 23, you're going to make some brand-new friends too!

And here's some great news: In heaven you'll even get along with and *love* people who maybe gave you a little trouble here on earth. Because in heaven everything is done perfectly! So even if you're not getting along with a friend (or brother or sister) right now, you'll be great friends up in heaven!

So a good way to practice for heaven is to try to get along with and love people around you right now. And if they don't know Jesus yet, let them know about Him and what He's done in your life already. That way they can get to know Him too and live forever in heaven with Him. And you!

32

I have a friend who goes to a different church than me. Will they still go to heaven?

You were all called together in one body to have peace.

Colossians 3:15

God has given us hundreds of churches that might be different in the way they worship, teach the Bible, or meet together. But as long as they love Jesus, believe in God's Word, and are obedient to God, they'll be growing closer to Him.

As far as whether your friend is going to heaven, that's a different question. Some people believe that if they go to church they're automatically going to heaven. Even in Jesus's time, some religious leaders thought that by following all the rules, they were a sure fit for eternity. But at the time, they were so busy trying to follow the rules, they missed having a friendship with Jesus.

Just because you show up at church every week doesn't make you a follower of Jesus any more than living in a garage makes you a car.

So if your friend has given their life over to Jesus and accepted His gift of being freed from the penalty of sin, then yes, you and your friend will enjoy heaven together forever.

As long as you, too, have said yes to Jesus! If you want to know how to become a follower of Jesus, check out the ABCs of friendship with Jesus on page 265.

If God is everywhere, why do we go to church?

They spent their time learning the apostles' teaching. And they continued to share, to break bread, and to pray together.

Acts 2:42

While it's true that God is everywhere and with us all the time, He still wants us to go to church whenever we can. Even though you can be best friends with God all by yourself, He created us to be with and around other people who love Him and who love us.

When we go to church or Sunday school, it gives us a chance to do three important things:

1. **Learn.** When we go to church, we get to learn more about God, Jesus, and the Bible. Usually, church services have a time when the pastor or Sunday school leader teaches about important Bible truths. This is really important because they've studied the Bible and can help us

understand what God is saying to us. God wants us to know Him, and by listening to older Christ followers, we'll learn more about how we can follow Him.

2. **Worship**. Another reason we go to church is because it gives us a chance to worship God with other people. You can always worship God on your own by thanking Him for the good things He's done for you or praising Him because He's amazing and can do anything, but it's fun to sing worship songs with other people at your church. It's important to worship God because He's worth it!

3. **Friendship**. By going to church you can connect with other Jesus followers. They might be members of your own family or friends or even people you haven't met before. And they can pray for you and help you get to know Jesus a little bit better. And who knows? You might end up helping and encouraging them!

So it's important to go to church whenever you can. If you don't belong to a church, ask your parents if they might help find one for your family. Look for a church that loves Jesus and believes in the Bible. Hopefully your church or kids' program is fun, interesting, and helps you grow in your friendship with God.

Why are there so many different churches?

A person's body is one thing, but it has many parts. Yes, there are many parts to a body, but all those parts make only one body. Christ is like that too.

1 Corinthians 12:12

There might be a lot of different churches in your town, and you might be wondering why. Why doesn't everybody who loves Jesus just meet in the same place? That way we could all be together. Is one of the churches right and the other ones wrong? No, not at all. Having different kinds of churches is part of God's plan to reach everybody.

From very early in the history of the Christian people, there have been different opinions of what a good church should be. Some people like a lot of music in their services while others have very little. Some think teaching is the most important thing while others think serving the community is what they should focus on. (Both are right!)

Some people like having their leaders run everything while other churches have a part for every member to play. So you see, since there are so many followers of Jesus around the world, there are going to be lots of ideas of what makes a good church.

Nowadays there are thousands of groups or denominations around the globe. And people can find a church that fits with what they believe as well as how they feel comfortable worshiping. God doesn't mind the different denominations as long as they all worship Him and love and care for one another.

What are your favorite things about your church? Friends? Music? The lessons? Snacks? If you don't go to church right now, what are some things you'd like to have at a church you would attend? Be creative! Use your imagination! A petting zoo? Free cupcakes? Fun music and games?

Were there girl Bible heroes or only guys?

"The Lord will let a woman defeat Sisera." So Deborah went with Barak to Kedesh.

Judges 4:9

Some people think the Bible is only about men—you know, stories about Moses, David, Daniel, Elijah, and Joshua. But if you really look at the Bible, you'll find lots of heroes that are women! Here are just a few.

Deborah

You can read about Deborah in the book of Judges, chapters 4 and 5. Deborah was a very wise woman and a prophetess, which means she heard messages from God and shared them with the people. During her time of judging Israel, a group of bad guys called the Canaanites, led by a king named Jabin and his general Sisera, came and attacked the Israelites over and over. They seemed unbeatable because they had nine hundred iron chariots!

(And Israel had none.) Finally, the Israelites cried out to God for help. Deborah told Barak, Israel's commander, that God wanted him to raise up an army and fight back against Jabin and Sisera. Barak said he would go, but only if Deborah would go with him. She agreed, and Barak gathered ten thousand men to fight with them. Once they arrived, Deborah encouraged Barak to attack, and he did. Then God did a miracle and caused a flood in the area where the battle was taking place. So the heavy iron chariots of the Canaanites were useless as their wheels stuck in the mud. Later, General Sisera escaped and was killed by another woman named Jael. Wow! Talk about hero women!

Is there someone in your life who encourages you? Who is it? And what are some ways you can be an encourager like Deborah?

Esther

This is another cool story, and you can read it in her very own book in the Old Testament, the book of Esther. Esther started out in life like a lot of people, a normal, unknown, young girl. But when she grew up, she became queen of Persia (it's a long story). While she was doing that, this really evil guy named Haman decided he wanted to do away with all of God's people—the Jews.

He had a plan all set up where anyone at all could attack their Jewish neighbor throughout the kingdom and the Jews couldn't do anything about it. Esther's cousin Mordecai persuaded Esther to go ask the king to change Haman's evil edict and save the people. At first Esther was scared; she knew that going before the king without an invitation could lead to the death penalty. But Mordecai told her that it might be for this very moment that she had become queen. So she risked it all and appeared before the king and persuaded him to write a new edict. Her bravery and obedience led to God saving the Jewish people. It's a great story; you should check it out.

What's the bravest thing you've ever done?

Mary Magdalene

Mary met Jesus when He helped her by getting rid of some bad spirits who were harassing her. After that moment, she knew she wanted to follow Him. She was one of the women who were standing by as Jesus hung on the cross, and she and some other women were the first to come to His tomb on Easter morning. And while she and the others were there, He came to them and showed them He was alive! Can you imagine how happy she must have been to see her Savior alive again? She ran to tell Jesus's disciples that He had risen, but they didn't believe her. Back then, people didn't take the word of a woman as seriously as that of a man, so isn't it cool that Jesus showed Himself to Mary before anyone else?

Some other girl heroes in the Bible include Mary, the mother of Jesus, who got an important message from an angel (Luke 2:26–38); Moses's mom, Jochebed, who saved him from Pharoah's plan to kill the Jewish babies (Exod. 2:1–10); a girl named Ruth, who left her home and family to follow God (Ruth 1:1–17); and Elizabeth, the mother of John the Baptist (Luke 1:23–25, 39–58).

So you see, God often uses ordinary people—boys *and* girls, to do great things for Him!

36

Does God always answer our prayers?

God listens to us every time we ask him. So we know
that he gives us the things that we ask from him.

1 John 5:15

The answer to this question is YES! God loves us and
always wants to answer our prayers.

But . . .

God loves us too much to give us everything we ask
the way we want it. Some people think God answers
prayers three ways:

1. **YES**—He might say "yes." We all love it when
   we ask God for something and He answers,
   especially right away. Maybe you prayed for
   someone to be healed or to make a new friend
   or even for God to help you not be anxious. And
   then He answered, and you could thank Him
   for hearing you and giving you what you needed
   at the time.

2. **NO**—God also answers our prayers sometimes by saying "no." What? That doesn't sound very good. But think about it: Even your parents don't say yes to everything you ask for.

   "Can we have cake and ice cream for dinner tonight?"

   "Will you send my brother or sister on a two-year around-the-world cruise?"

   "Can I have a pony?"

   Some things that seem important at the time aren't really good for you in the long run. God always knows what's best for us and will only give us those things.

3. **WAIT**—Sometimes when we pray, God's answer is "wait." God is waiting for us to be ready for the answer to come. He might know we're not ready yet (*"Hey, God, can I start driving?"*) or that the answer won't be good for us right now (*"God, I sure could use a million dollars"*). It doesn't mean God isn't listening or that He doesn't care; it's just that He's waiting for the perfect time to answer.

So what do we do in the meantime? If you really feel like your prayer is a good one and that it's important, KEEP PRAYING!

God might be teaching you to trust Him even when you don't see the answer to your prayers right away. Remember, God's top priority is friendship with you. So He'll do whatever it takes to make sure you two are close. Keep talking to Him whenever you can.

You might even ask Him to help you pray. Jesus's friends did that (Luke 11:1). Don't forget, praying is just talking to God.

TALK IT OVER

"God? Are You Listening?"

Have you ever prayed and prayed for something, and God didn't seem to answer? That can be frustrating. The last chapter said that God answers our prayers with either a "yes," a "no," or "wait." Here are some questions to discuss about how and why God doesn't always answer our prayers the way we want:

1. Are you praying for something right now and God hasn't answered yet? What is it and what do you think is going on?

2. Sometimes God wants us to wait before He answers our prayers. What are some reasons He might want you to do that?

3. Is it ever okay to tell God that you're disappointed because He didn't answer your prayer?

What are some things you need to pray about right now? God doesn't need us to use special words or phrases when we pray. He wants us to be open and honest and to tell Him what's on our hearts. Read Psalm 62:8 to see what He means.

37

Will we have emotions in heaven?

> Let us rejoice and be happy
> and give God glory!
>
> Revelation 19:7

You might keep hearing that there won't be any fear, jealousy, or anger in heaven, but does that mean we won't feel any emotions? No, not at all. We'll have all kinds of good feelings, like love, joy, excitement, and peace. Have you ever been with a friend or family member doing something fun and having a great time? Or have you gone to the park, the beach, the zoo, or a friend's house and enjoyed yourself like crazy? Those are happy emotions, and you'll experience those all the time when you're in heaven.

Emotions we won't experience up there are loneliness, fear, anxiety, and sadness. After all, how can you be sad or afraid when you're hanging out with Jesus? And there won't be any more anger or jealousy either because we'll all be happy and content with everything God has for us.

So if you want to bring a little heaven to earth right now, practice not letting your negative emotions run your life. Do you get mad easily? Are you jealous of somebody? Do you talk behind their back? Ask God to help you change your thinking and start to let some of those hard feelings go.

Emotions aren't bad by themselves, but when they start to hurt us or other people, we might need to control them. And with God's help we can!

Will we be able to fly in heaven?

I said, "I wish I had wings like a dove.
Then I would fly away and rest."

Psalm 55:6

Wouldn't it be cool if you could fly? Just take off like Superman or the Green Lantern? Get wherever you want without worrying about traffic congestion or even using streets?

Since heaven is going to be totally different than earth, there's a good chance we'll be able to fly up there. Since we'll be outside of earth's atmosphere—and *time*, for that matter—we'll be able to do lots of things we can't do here. And flying just might be one of them.

After Jesus was crucified and rose from the dead, He led His disciples up onto a mountain to say goodbye to them. Then He was lifted up into the sky until a cloud covered Him and He went to heaven. So I guess Jesus was flying in a sense. And maybe, just maybe, we'll be able to fly in heaven too.

Do people in heaven see what's going on here on earth?

> Then two men were talking with Jesus. The men were Moses and Elijah. They appeared in heavenly glory, talking with Jesus about his death which would happen in Jerusalem.
>
> Luke 9:30–31

Even though we can't tell from the Bible exactly if the people who have gone on before us to heaven can see what's happening here on earth, there are a couple verses that might help us.

First, in the book of Hebrews, chapter 12, we read that we have a lot of people watching us live out our lives for God. Who are these people? According to the chapter before that—chapter 11—the people might be thousands of God's followers who have gone on before us. If that's so, then yes, they're in heaven watching and cheering for us. That's cool.

But there are also people around us right now, our pastors, leaders, and other Christians in our lives, who are also watching and encouraging us, especially when we're going through hard times.

In Luke 9:30–31, we see Jesus talking to Moses and Elijah (both of whom have died and gone on to heaven). What are they talking about? They're discussing that Jesus is about to go to the cross and then on to heaven. So it seems like they are aware of what is going on here on earth.

It's a comforting thought that people who have died and gone to heaven might be aware of all we're doing here, isn't it?

A Heavenly Audience

It's kind of fun and interesting to think that maybe your grandfather or other ancestors are watching you from heaven. But one thing we do know for sure is that God is always watching you and cares about every little thing you do.

1. If you could go back and witness a famous historical event, what would it be?

2. If you could meet a famous historical person, who would that be?

3. Even though we're not sure if people in heaven are watching us, we do know that the people who are around us every day are. What are some ways you can show God's love to people as you live out your life at school, at home, and in your neighborhood?

4. Is there someone in your life who encourages you in your friendship with Jesus? It might be a parent, a pastor, a Sunday school teacher, or a good friend. What do you like about them?

Pray for a friend or family member today who may not know Jesus yet.

Who was Moses?

Moses lifted up the snake in the desert. It is the same with the Son of Man. The Son of Man must be lifted up too.

John 3:14

In the book of Exodus in the Old Testament, we meet a guy named Moses. He was Jewish, a follower of God, and believe it or not, ended up as the adopted grandson of Pharaoh, the king of Egypt. When Moses grew up, God called him to lead the Jewish people out of Egypt where they'd been slaves for four hundred years. God wanted Moses to lead them into the promised land—the nation we call Israel today.

Even though Moses was scared to do it, he trusted God, and with God's amazing help, Moses led the people away from Egypt and off into the wilderness. The hike should have taken less than a month, but because of the people's disobedience and rebellion, the trip ended up taking forty years!

Moses is probably the most famous name in the Old Testament and definitely a major hero of the Jewish people.

Through Moses, God opened the Red Sea so the people could pass through. God fed them every day with manna, bread from heaven, and even gave Moses the Ten Commandments so the people would know how God wanted them to live and treat one another.

Moses wasn't always a strong leader. In fact, he tried to talk God out of using him to lead the Israelites! But Moses learned to trust God, and soon he watched God do some amazing things. Read all about Moses in the Old Testament book of Exodus.

I'm just a kid; why should I be thinking about heaven?

You have known the Holy Scriptures since you were a child. The Scriptures are able to make you wise. And that wisdom leads to salvation through faith in Christ Jesus.

2 Timothy 3:15

That's a really good question—I mean, don't most people think about heaven when they get to be really old, like forty? Why should you, a young kid, think about it?

One reason God would like you to think about heaven is because, believe it or not, what you understand about heaven and how you're going to live forever with God will affect how you live your life here right now.

Really? How?

Well, when you live knowing that your life here on earth is just the beginning of your forever life, you look at things a lot differently. You might begin to realize that a lot of the stuff that seems so important right now isn't all that important compared to what God has planned for you in the future. Like hurts and disappointments. Things that really hurt right now might not seem important when you realize that heaven's going to be perfect, with no more pain or loss or disappointment.

And remember, God loves you and has only good plans for you. (Check out Jeremiah 29:11 in the Old Testament.)

Also, when we live with an eye toward God and heaven, we can make better decisions. Decisions that won't hurt us or the people around us. Because we know we belong to God and that He's preparing us to live forever with Him. So even if you're just a kid right now, you can be assured that God's plans for you stretch all the way into eternity!

Is heaven just like earth? What's the difference?

> Then I saw a new heaven and a new earth. The first heaven and the first earth had disappeared. . . . "[God] will wipe away every tear from their eyes. There will be no more death, sadness, crying, or pain. All the old ways are gone."
>
> Revelation 21:1, 4

As we talked about earlier, movies and TV shows often show heaven as clouds and blue skies and people dressed in robes, sometimes even strumming harps. Frankly, it looks kind of boring. But heaven isn't going to be like that at all. Heaven's going to be the most incredible place you can ever imagine.

Think about how creative God is—after all, He came up with the idea of oceans and rivers and lakes, mountains, whales, polar bears, tigers, and penguins. If He made the earth this incredible, think about how amazing heaven's going to be!

If there are mountains there, they'll be taller and more beautiful than any here on earth. If there are lakes, they'll be bluer and clearer, and if there are oceans, they'll be deeper and more full of life than the ones we know. And no pollution! There might be jungles and forests and maybe even wide, long rivers.

But the main difference between earth and heaven is that in heaven there's no more sin. That's the Bible word for bad stuff. Think about it for a moment.

There won't be any hurt feelings. Nobody will ever be left out, made fun of, or bullied.

There won't be any sickness. No cancer. Or pain. Or headaches. Or stubbed toes or bee stings.

There won't be any fights, arguments, jealousy, stealing, or shame.

And best of all, there won't be any more death. Everyone in heaven is going to live forever with God and Jesus. So no; heaven is going to be so much more incredible and awesome than anything we know of earth. And God will be there with us!

Could Jesus really control the weather?

He made the storm be still.
He calmed the waves.

Psalm 107:29

In Luke 8:22–25, Jesus does one of His most awesome miracles. He and His disciples got into a fishing boat and started heading across the Sea of Galilee, a small sea sometimes called the Lake of Gennesaret. Jesus must have been pretty tired that day, because after a few minutes he curled up on a cushion in the back of the boat and fell asleep. Things were going pretty well until they reached the middle of the lake. Suddenly, the wind picked up, the sky grew dark, and the water became choppy and rough. Pretty soon, Jesus and His disciples were in a full-blown storm! The waves were sloshing water into the boat, the rain poured down, and the soaked disciples were getting scared. Remember, some of these guys were fishermen who'd spent their whole lives on the water, so this must have been one scary storm! They looked toward the back of the boat, and what did they see? Jesus was still asleep on the cushion. They rushed over to Him, woke Him up, and said, "Master, we're going down! We're all gonna die!" or words to that effect.

Jesus woke from His sleep, made His way to the front of the boat, and shouted at the storm, "Peace, calm down!" or something like that, and guess what? Immediately, the wind died down. The rain stopped and the water instantly became calm and flat. Jesus turned to the guys and said, "Where is your faith?" It was like He was saying that they'd put their faith in the wind because they'd seen what it could do. They had faith in the rain to get them wet and faith in the waves to rock the boat. They really believed they were done for.

But Jesus wanted them to put their faith in *Him* and know that He wasn't going to let anything happen to His friends.

Afterward, the disciples looked at each other and said, "Who is this guy? Even the winds and the water obey Him!" They might have even remembered the words of Psalm 107:29—"He made the storm be still. He calmed the waves"—and realized that Jesus wasn't just a good teacher or a good friend; He was God Himself.

TALK IT OVER

The Disciples' Scary Boat Trip

Jesus did some pretty awesome things while He was here on earth—healed the sick, cured the blind, and raised the dead—but this is one of His most spectacular miracles. Can you believe He spoke to the weather and it obeyed Him?

1. When He and His disciples started out on their trip across the Sea of Galilee, Jesus went to the back of the boat and fell asleep. Why do you suppose He did that?

2. Do you think the disciples felt seasick during this trip? Have you ever felt seasick?

3. Why do you suppose the disciples wanted to wake Jesus up? Do you think they wanted Him to help somehow? What do you think they wanted Him to do?

4. If the disciples knew Psalm 107:29 (see above), what do you think they thought about Jesus when He spoke to the storm and it calmed down?

5. In what ways do you think the disciples were different when they got to the other side of the lake from how they were when they started their trip?

6. Do you believe God is powerful enough to fix any problem in your life?

Hopefully this story reminds you of how powerful God is. Are you going through something right now that you could use God's help with? Take some time to pray for God to help you. Also, is there someone you know who needs God's help? Pray for them too.

He's powerful enough to help you with anything!

Who was Samson? How did he get so strong?

The Spirit of the Lord entered Samson and gave him great power.

Judges 14:19

Samson was one of God's special people back in the Old Testament. You can read about him in Judges 13–16. It's quite a wild story. Samson was set apart to serve God in an unusual way even before he was born!

God's people were in trouble with some enemies called the Philistines. So God instructed Samson to help Israel and defeat the Philistines. We're not sure if Samson was really big and strong on his own from his upbringing and maybe lots of physical labor while he was growing up. But even if that was the case, the real secret of Samson's amazing strength came not from his own ability but from the Spirit of the Lord (Judg. 13:25).

Whenever Samson was called upon to fight the Philistines, God sent His Spirit to fill and empower Samson in order to bring about the victory. And the Spirit of God is pretty powerful! Samson had some interesting and amazing victories. One time the bad guys tied him up, but he broke free from the ropes and killed a thousand Philistines with a donkey's jawbone. Whoa.

But in spite of Samson's strength, he didn't always obey God, and as a result, God took His Spirit (and Samson's power) away from him. Samson ended up getting caught by the Philistines, put in prison, and eventually dying. But right before Samson died, he knocked down a building with three thousand evil Philistines in it, so even in his last moments he helped Israel defeat their enemies.

Samson's Special Vow

Samson's parents dedicated Samson to the Lord even before he was born. As a result, he took a Nazirite vow, which meant he wasn't supposed to drink wine, he was never to touch a dead body, and he was never to cut his hair. Can you imagine how long his hair must have been after a few years? How often do you cut your hair?

DID YOU KNOW?

Even though the Bible was written over two thousand years ago, there are some phrases from it we still use today.

"Handwriting on the Wall"

When you hear someone say they're reading the handwriting on the wall, it means that they see something coming in the future that might not be good. For example, "When John saw people losing their jobs, he saw the handwriting on the wall that he might be next." This phrase comes from the story in the book of Daniel, chapter 5, about an evil king who saw a mysterious hand writing a warning message to him *on the wall*!

So they brought the gold cups. They had been taken from the Temple of God in Jerusalem. And the king and his royal guests, his wives and his slave women drank from them. As they were drinking, they praised their gods. Those gods were made from gold, silver, bronze, iron, wood and stone.

Then suddenly a person's hand appeared. The fingers wrote words on the plaster on the wall. This was near the lampstand in the royal palace. The king watched the hand as it wrote. (vv. 3–5)

"Labor of Love"

When you hear this phrase, it means that even though something might be hard work, the person is doing it out of love. For example, "He didn't mind mowing his grandma's lawn; it was a labor of love." This phrase comes from 1 Thessalonians 1:3:

> . . . remembering without ceasing your work of faith, *labor of love*, and patience of hope in our Lord Jesus Christ in the sight of our God and Father. (NKJV, emphasis added)

"Rise and Shine"

This phrase means it's time to get up and start a brand-new day! Your mom or dad might say this to you in the morning. It comes from Isaiah 60:1:

> Arise, shine;
> For your light has come!
> And the glory of the Lord is risen upon you.
> (NKJV)

My friend told me we'll have mansions in heaven. Is that true?

In my Father's house are many mansions: if it were not so, I would have told you.

John 14:2 KJV

Your friend was probably referring to the verse mentioned above. So that sounds like we'll be living in big, fancy houses once we get to heaven.

Sounds cool. Maybe they'll have seventy rooms, movie theaters, bowling alleys, swimming pools, and even tennis courts!

Or maybe not. The actual word Jesus uses in this passage doesn't necessarily mean big mansions, like where movie stars or rock singers live. The word could mean dwelling places. So in other words, the verse might say, "In My Father's house, there are many places to dwell (to stay), and I'm going to prepare one for you." In Old English, the word *mansion* could mean room or place to live.

But since we know that Jesus never does anything halfway, while we might not be getting actual mansions in heaven, you can be sure that wherever we're going to be staying will be amazing. And because He says that He *personally* will be preparing them for us, you know they're going to be awesome!

Grab a piece of paper and draw a picture of a house you'd like to live in. It might be a huge mansion or a tiny, cozy little place. What are some of the things you'd like to have in there? Ice cream store? Swimming pool? Game room? Horse stable?

Will we sleep in heaven?

I go to bed and sleep in peace.
Lord, only you keep me safe.

Psalm 4:8

God created sleep for us here on earth because He knows we get tired! God's put together cycles in our lives. In fact, you can see them all around you: day and night; winter, spring, summer, and fall; and sleeping and waking. He put these all together because He knew we needed to rest and recover from our work and play. We think better and feel better when we've gotten enough sleep.

But in heaven we're going to have new bodies that will never get tired. So we won't have the same need or desire for sleep that we do here on earth.

Also, there's a verse in the book of Revelation (the last book in the Bible) that says, "There will never be night again. They will not need the light of a lamp or the light of the sun. The Lord God will give them light" (22:5). So if there's no night, it seems like there won't be a need or a time for sleep.

God does want us to rest, though, so who knows? Maybe we will get to sleep in heaven occasionally. But maybe it'll be okay to stay up a little later there, and maybe get one more glass of water before we go to bed.

DID YOU KNOW?

When you read the story of the shepherd boy David fighting a giant, it might sound like a fairy tale. (You can read it in 1 Sam. 17.) After all, wasn't there a giant in the story of Jack and the Beanstalk?

But this giant, whose name was Goliath, was a real person. In fact, there are several giants mentioned in the Old Testament. But even though Goliath was a really big dude, he wasn't as big as the giants in fairy tales. The Bible says he was "six cubits and a span" (1 Sam. 17:4 KJV). Since a cubit was probably around eighteen inches, that would make the guy nine feet nine inches—almost ten feet—tall! So David really had to trust God to stand up against this guy.

Read about other giants, including Goliath's brothers, in these passages:

Deuteronomy 3:11
2 Samuel 21:20
1 Chronicles 20:5–8

If heaven's so great, is this life not important?

Teach us to number our days,
    that we may gain a heart of wisdom.

Psalm 90:12 NIV

With all this talk about heaven, you could start to get the idea that it's so great up there, we don't need to think that much about life here and now. But even though heaven's going to be, like, forever and it's going to be amazing, Jesus never said that our lives right here and now aren't important. Just the opposite! Psalm 90 tells us to "number our days." That simply means to make the best use of our time here in this life. We're to appreciate every day that God gives us. When we do that, we give God a chance to develop in us a heart of wisdom. And who doesn't want that?

God put us here on earth at this time for some good reasons. Here are just a few to think about:

1. Throughout our life, we have the chance to get to know God—what He's like, how much He loves us, and how He'd like us to live.

2. A second reason this life is so important is because it gives us a chance to become more and more like Jesus. Even though we'll never, ever be as perfect as He is, we still can become more and more like Him every day. Think about it: What are things about Jesus we'd like in our lives? His love for others, His patience, His wisdom, His peace. As we grow, we might even begin to see other people the way He sees them.

3. One other thing God wants us to do while we're here is to pray for other people and let them know about Jesus. Who knows? That person might be a friend, a teacher, or even the person who drives the school bus.

Even though heaven's going to be amazing, God has us here on earth for some really important reasons. So don't miss out. Ask Him how He'd like you to become more and more like Jesus today.

Making the Best Use of Our Time

You may not be thinking much about heaven right now—after all, you're still a kid—but knowing that heaven is going to be our forever home can help us live our lives in ways that make God happy.

1. What are some ways we can live our lives for God right now?
2. When Jesus was here on earth, He did lots of cool things, like healing the sick, walking on water, and even calming a storm! While you probably won't do things exactly the way Jesus did, what are some ways you can help somebody you know get to know Him?
3. How does knowing that heaven is going to be our forever home make a difference in your life right now?
4. How can you make the best use of your time right now?

PS: When God tells us to number our days, that includes resting! Make sure you get a good night's sleep every night and that you take one day off a week. God wants us to learn to rest in Him!

What about people who have never heard of Jesus? What happens to them?

> But since the beginning of the world those things have been easy to understand. They are made clear by what God has made.
>
> Romans 1:20

Lots of people have asked this question for thousands of years. If God is fair, how can He not let someone into heaven who's never heard of Jesus?

Well, we need to remember that God is perfect. He loves all of us—even people who have never heard about Him. And we can trust Him to do the right thing.

Here are a couple things to remember when we think about this question:

1. God is always fair, just, and kind. Unlike us, God knows what's going on inside of every person in the world, and He'll always do the right thing.

2. We can also trust that God can reveal Himself to people in any way He wants. Romans 1:19–20 says, "Yes, God has clearly shown them everything that may be known about him. There are things about God that people cannot see—his eternal power and all the things that make him God. But since the beginning of the world those things have been easy to understand. They are made clear by what God has made."

   In other words, people who have never had the chance to hear the good news of Jesus can still look around at the mountains, oceans, rivers, stars, animals, and even each other and realize that somebody pretty big created all of it. If they're aware of this and seek Him, God will be faithful to reveal Himself to them. Jeremiah 29:13 says that if we seek God with all our heart, He'll be found by us.

3. And the awesome thing about God is that even though He knows whether we're going to choose to follow Him or not, He gives us the free choice to do what we want to do.

   He doesn't ever force anyone to love or follow Him. He leaves it up to us. That's how much He loves us.

So what do we do? We need to follow God, make sure we obey Him, and let other people know that God loves them and Jesus died for them. If we love people and show God's love to them, we'll be helping introduce people to Him.

Here's a fun thing you can do as a family: Get ahold of a map of the world and choose a country to start praying for. Read a little bit about the country to help you know how to pray.

Or you might just get a map of the city or town in which you live and start praying for it. Don't forget to pray for schools, hospitals, businesses, and your city leaders.

Where do we get all these answers about heaven? How do we know any of this stuff?

> God's word is true.
>> Everything he does is right.
>>> Psalm 33:4

Lots of people have lots of ideas about heaven. Some think we'll be sitting on clouds strumming harps. Some think it'll be an endless party and some people think it might be boring. So how do we get the best answers about heaven? By checking out the Bible—God's Word to us.

While the Bible doesn't tell us everything about heaven, it's the most reliable and truthful source we can get. And since God wrote it Himself, we can believe that what's in there is true.

Wait, what? God wrote the Bible? I thought people wrote it!

You're right. But God wrote it *through* people! God picked forty different authors: some leaders, some kings, and some fishermen or tax collectors. And all of them helped write the sixty-six little books that make up the one big book we call the Bible. So how can we know we can trust what's in there? There are a couple ways:

1. **Archaeology.** There are people who study ancient times. They're called archaeologists. They travel all over to discover old bones, houses, and sometimes even entire towns. They spend months and months digging up relics in places all over the world. Some of these people work in Israel, where most of the Bible takes place. And they've uncovered all kinds of things that help prove what the Bible says. They've found mentions of David (remember David and Goliath?) and Pontius Pilate, the governor who sentenced Jesus to death. They've discovered the pool where Jesus healed the blind man, and King Hezekiah's water tunnel mentioned in 2 Kings 20:20. They may have even found the house of Jesus's good friend Peter and lots of other things mentioned in the Old and New Testaments. This helps show us that the Bible is true and reliable.

2. **Prophecy.** *Prophecy* just means that people predicted certain events years or even centuries in advance and the events came true. For example,

the Old Testament was written hundreds of years before Jesus came, and yet, some of the writers told us things that He would do, down to the smallest detail. There are other examples in which the writers predicted things that affected God's people, Israel, and even world events. So, because these things came true, in some ways the Bible proves itself!

3. **Matching manuscripts.** What does that mean? It means that as more and more early copies of Scripture are found (sometimes written on papyrus or sheepskin), they match the Scriptures we have now. Some of these copies are more than a thousand years old and show that no big, important changes have been made since they were first written. We now have over five thousand early manuscripts of the Scriptures.

Whenever you have big questions about God, Jesus, or heaven, it's always a good idea to check out what the Bible has to say about it. That's one way God speaks to us.

Some Prophecies about Jesus in the Old Testament

Prophecy	When It Came True
Psalm 2:7: Jesus would be declared the Son of God.	Matthew 3:16–17
Psalm 78:2–4: He'll teach using parables.	Matthew 13:10–15
Isaiah 7:14: He'll be born of a virgin.	Luke 1:34
Isaiah 53:4–6: He'll be a sacrifice for our sins.	Romans 5:6–10
Micah 5:2: He'll be born in Bethlehem.	Matthew 2:1
Zechariah 9:9: He'll enter Jerusalem on a donkey.	John 12:14–15

Who wrote the Bible?

Every word of God can be trusted.
He protects those who come to him for safety.

Proverbs 30:5

The Bible is a really special book. It truly is God's Word; in fact, some people call it God's love letter to all of us. God used forty different writers to write the sixty-six books that make up the one book—the Bible. Some of these writers were kings, like David and Solomon. One was a doctor named Luke. Some worked as servants to royalty, like a guy named Nehemiah, and some were God's spokesmen, called prophets, like Samuel, Isaiah, Jeremiah, and Ezekiel. God would speak to them, and they would pass the message on to the people. Some Bible writers ran away from God, like Jonah, and one New Testament writer started out trying to arrest Jesus's followers and stop the spread of Christianity. His name was Paul, and he ended up meeting Jesus face-to-face and then helping to spread Christianity all over the world at that time.

Some of the Bible's books are poetry, like the Psalms and Song of Solomon. Some are history, like the first and second books of Samuel and Kings in the Old Testament. The New Testament is focused on Jesus: what He did, what He taught, and how He died and rose again. Some of the New Testament teaches us about Jesus's early followers, and then there are also letters that help us know how to live our lives. Then the very last book of the Bible is called Revelation, and the events mentioned in it haven't even happened yet! It was written by one of Jesus's friends, a guy named John.

It's good to read the Bible to get to know God and Jesus. There is a simple reading plan at the end of this book that'll help you get started in the book of Mark from the New Testament.

TALK IT OVER

God's Love Letter—the Bible

Even though lots of people have tried to disprove what the Bible says, nobody ever has. It's one of the oldest books in the world, and even though it's been translated into hundreds of languages, the message is still the same— God loves you and He's got good things planned for you!

1. Why do you think God gave us the Bible?
2. Name some good things that come from reading God's Word.
3. If you were God, how would you let people know what you were like? (Hint: He gave us His Word, and He sent Jesus to come show us what God the Father was like.)
4. Why do you think it's important for us to read the Bible? Do you think it's a good idea to read a little at a time?

There are lots of Bible translations around. Some Bibles have pictures and are written for kids your age, and some even have notes or devotionals that help you understand what's going on in the stories. Make sure the Bible you're reading is simple to understand and just right for your age group.

What's the difference between the Old Testament and the New Testament?

How do we know that we love God's children? We know because we love God and we obey his commands.

1 John 5:2

This is a great question. Most books aren't divided into two parts, are they? The simple answer is that the Old Testament is the story of God's people from the very beginning of time. In fact, the first words in the Bible are "In the beginning . . ."

The Old Testament starts with the creation of the world and goes through the stories of heroes and leaders like Noah, Abraham, Moses, Joshua, David, Solomon, and a whole bunch of kings. It tells the story of how God's people spent four hundred years as slaves in Egypt before God used Moses to lead them out of that country and into the promised land, which we now know as

Israel. And all the time the people were waiting for their promised One—God's Son, Jesus.

The New Testament takes over the story with what are called the Gospels (*gospel* means good news), Matthew, Mark, Luke, and John, and they focus on telling the story of Jesus. We learn about His birth in a stable in Bethlehem, how He grew up, and how He was baptized by His cousin John the Baptist. We read about how Jesus taught people about God, healed them, and did a bunch of miracles. Then we read about how He died, was raised from the dead (wow!), and went to heaven. The book of Acts tells the stories of Jesus's followers, and then there are letters written by some of these followers, including Peter, John, James, and a guy named Paul.

And the book of Revelation talks about when Jesus will come back and the world will be perfect again!

Whew, that's a quick explanation of the Old and New Testaments, but hopefully it helps you see what they're all about.

DID YOU KNOW?

Probably the strangest job we see in the Bible is the job of being a professional mourner. These were people who would come over when someone died, and they would cry and wail and generally act really sad. And sometimes they were real loud. And they actually got paid for this!

Here are a few verses that mention professional mourners:

Matthew 9:23

Jesus continued along with the ruler and went into the ruler's house. Jesus saw people there who play music for funerals. And he saw many people there crying.

Amos 5:16

This is what the Lord, the Lord God of heaven's armies, says:

"People will be crying in all the public places.
They will be saying, 'Oh, no!' in the streets.

> They will call the farmers to come and
> weep.
> They will pay people to cry out loud for
> them."

Jeremiah 9:17

This is what the Lord of heaven's armies says:

> "Now, think about these things!
> Call for the women who cry at funerals.
> Send for those women who are good
> at that job."

Are the stories in the Bible for real or are they made up?

Make them ready for your service through your truth. Your teaching is truth.

John 17:17

If you're like most kids, you've heard lots of made-up stories growing up. Stories like *Cinderella*, *Snow White*, *Beauty and the Beast*, and even stories of superheroes like Spider-Man, Superman, and Wonder Woman. And if you've ever read the Bible, you've got to admit it's full of some pretty amazing stories. They almost sound like fairy tales.

The story of God opening up the Red Sea so the people could walk through! A kid fighting a giant and a guy being swallowed by a fish! All of these sound pretty unbelievable. But guess what? The stories in the Bible are for real. They're all true!

Even though each story teaches us a lesson, like learning to trust God or having faith or stepping out to do something He tells us to do, they're real stories that actually happened.

We know this because God is always truthful, so He wouldn't tell us something that was a lie.

And you know who else believed the stories in the Bible? Jesus. Jesus Himself talked about the Scriptures and showed that He trusted them. Of course, the Scriptures He was talking about back then were what we now call the Old Testament, because the New Testament hadn't been written yet. But Jesus quoted the Old Testament all the time and talked about King David, Jonah and the big fish, Moses and the burning bush, and the bread from heaven that was given to the people when they left Egypt. He also talked about the big flood and how God saved Noah and his family. In fact, at one worship service, Jesus even read from the Old Testament book of Isaiah.

So yes, Jesus believed the Bible. And you can too!

What else do I need to know about the Bible?

Your word is like a lamp for my feet
and a light for my way.

Psalm 119:105

Did you know that the Bible is the bestselling book of all time? Over five billion people currently have access to a Bible. It's an unusual book because it's actually a library of books written by more than forty authors over a period of 1,500 years! Here are a few questions you might have about God's Word, the Bible:

Was the Bible originally written in English? No, the Old Testament part of the Bible was originally written in Hebrew, the language of God's people, the Jews. The New Testament was mostly written in Greek, one of the major languages during the time of Jesus and after.

How many languages has the Bible been translated into? The entire Bible has been translated into more than 700 languages, and portions of the Bible into at least 3,500 languages.

How do I read the Bible? The Bible is different from most books that you read from the very first page. You can do that with the Bible—in fact, the first chapter talks about when God created the whole world—but if you're new to the Bible, the best way to start out is by reading one of the Gospels. These are the first four books of the New Testament, and they're all about Jesus. There are four Gospels, Matthew, Mark, Luke, and John, and they tell of all that Jesus taught and did and how He died and rose again.

A great way to start reading the Bible is to take a few minutes every day, maybe first thing in the morning or right before bed, and read a few verses. At the end of this book, there is a Bible reading plan that'll help you get started.

54

Will there be banks in heaven? How about money?

Give this command to those who are rich with things of this world. Tell them not to be proud. Tell them to hope in God, not their money. Money cannot be trusted, but God takes care of us richly. He gives us everything to enjoy.

1 Timothy 6:17

While we can't be completely sure if there will be money in heaven, there doesn't seem to be any need for it. It appears that everything we'll need will be provided for us by God Himself. And when God does something, you know it's going to be AWESOME.

Jesus talks about a big banquet in Luke 14:16–17, so we know we'll have all the food we could possibly eat. And in John 14:2–3, He promises He'll prepare a place for the disciples (and us!) to stay, so we know that'll be way cool. And we won't even have to pay rent!

There probably won't be any banks in heaven, so we can add another one to our list of jobs we won't need in heaven—bankers.

Jesus talked a lot about money while He was here on earth. He never said that money, or even having money, was wrong but to make sure our love of money never becomes more important than our friendship with Him. We'll talk about that in the next question.

Jesus wants us to always remember that God is going to take care of all our needs here and in heaven.

Did Jesus say that being rich will keep you from going to heaven?

> Then Jesus said to his followers, "I tell you the truth. It will be very hard for a rich person to enter the kingdom of heaven."
>
> Matthew 19:23

Actually, Jesus never said being rich keeps you from going to heaven. In Matthew, Mark, and Luke, He said it's *hard* for a rich person to enter heaven. He said this after talking to a rich, young guy who had gone away and decided not to follow Jesus.

So what did Jesus mean by that? It seems that He was saying that sometimes we depend on our riches to bring us happiness and forget that our biggest need in life is a friendship with God through Jesus.

But guess what? *Riches* can mean more than money. *Wait, what? What does that mean?*

Well, *riches* can be anything we depend on to make our life full while forgetting how good God is to us. We might depend on friends or our abilities—whether in sports, art, music, or school. We might think our house makes us special or our clothes or even the grades we get.

But listen, not one of those things is bad, including money or even being rich. Our problems begin when we forget about God and start to depend on other things to make us happy in life instead of Him.

So what do we do? First, make sure your friendship with Jesus is the most important thing in your life. Then you might get to do all these things—sports, work, music, art, even making money—because you'll always remember that every one of these things is a gift from God. And He wants you to enjoy them and use them to help other people and to make God shine in your life.

Can even really bad people, like murderers, go to heaven?

But Christ died for us while we were still sinners. In this way God shows his great love for us.

Romans 5:8

The short answer to this question is yes. No matter how bad a person has been or what bad things they've done, if they're truly sorry, they stop doing those things and let God know they need His forgiveness (the Bible calls this "repentance"). He will forgive them, and they can enter heaven. In fact, you might be surprised by who's up in heaven once you get there.

But this repentance, or change of heart, needs to be for real. Lots and lots of really bad people have been forgiven by God because He loves all of us and wants all of us to spend forever with Him in heaven. There was even a guy in the Bible who hunted down Christians and had some of them killed. But when he met Jesus, he really changed and in fact became one of Jesus's top followers.

He even ended up writing a lot of the New Testament. His name is Paul.

And remember the guy hanging on the cross next to Jesus who had led a really bad life? When he asked Jesus to remember him, Jesus assured him that they would be in paradise together—that day!

So does this mean I can do anything I want and God will forgive me? Well, yes, He'll forgive you, but why would you want to do something that would hurt other people and even yourself? We'll talk more about that later.

When you start a friendship with God, you will, with His help, begin to change for the better. Slowly, it'll become easier for you to obey Him and make good choices. Ask God to help you. If you're sometimes tempted to do bad stuff, like lie or hurt somebody with your words or actions, He'll help you stop doing it. But be patient. Sometimes it takes a while, but God wants you to be successful. Ask Him to help you live a life that makes Him look good.

Who was David?
Was he for real?

David was the youngest son. Jesse's three oldest sons
followed Saul.

1 Samuel 17:14

One of the coolest people we meet in the Old Testament is a guy by the name of David. When we first meet him, he's pretty young, maybe just a little bit older than you.

David was the youngest of seven brothers, and their father was named Jesse. They lived in a town called Bethlehem. (Yup, the same town where Jesus was born around a thousand years later.) David's job was to take care of the sheep. And while he was out there, he fought a lion and a bear (not at the same time) to protect the sheep. It was out in the fields where David also wrote a bunch of poems called psalms. One day a prophet by the name of Samuel came to town and declared David king of Israel. Can you imagine how this went over with his brothers? After all, David was just a young kid at that point.

But then David had to wait somewhere between twelve and fifteen years to actually become king. Talk about being patient! Yeah, he didn't become king until he was thirty. Meanwhile, David went through some pretty hard stuff. He fought a giant named Goliath (check out that story in 1 Sam. 17), and he was chased around by the current king of Israel, a guy named Saul who wanted to kill him.

Finally, after Saul died, David was declared king of Israel. But his troubles didn't stop then. He was constantly fighting Israel's enemies, especially a nasty group of people called the Philistines. And later in David's life, his own son rebelled against him and almost took the kingdom away from him.

David had good times and bad times. There were even times when he disappointed God and had to come and confess his wrongs. But the good news is God forgave him and gave him a long life, and David became known as the greatest king of Israel. In fact, one of Jesus's titles when He was walking around on earth was Jesus, Son of David.

It's pretty interesting that God used a young shepherd boy to lead the entire country of Israel. Can you ever see God using you to do something really big and important?

What's a really big thing you'd like to do for God?

Will we ever be afraid in heaven?

Where God's love is, there is no fear, because God's perfect love takes away fear.

1 John 4:18

Since we've lived in this world all our lives and it seems like we've always had something to be afraid of, it just seems to follow that fear will follow *us* to heaven.

But here's some good—no, great—news. There won't be any fear in heaven! For one thing, you'll be with God in person, so you'll know you've always got somebody to guard you and protect you from anything bad.

And since God is with you and loves you, you'll have no reason to fear. In fact, 1 John 4:18 says, "Perfect love"—and who has more perfect love than God?—"takes away fear." And when we're right there with God, living in His perfect love, it's pretty much guaranteed—there won't be any room for fear.

But here's some more great news. There won't ever be anything *to fear* in heaven!

So whatever scares you—wars, hurricanes, fights, robberies, monsters, being separated from your family—not to worry; those things won't be happening in heaven. And if you're afraid of strangers, don't worry; there won't be any strangers in heaven. We'll all be one big family!

So the answer to your question is no. You won't have any reason to be afraid or anxious because heaven's going to be awesome and wonderful, with no fear and no reason to fear.

What are some things you might be afraid of?

How can God help you right now to reduce your fears? It might involve asking other people to help you too.

Who was John the Baptist? Did he really eat bugs?

John was baptizing people in the desert. He preached a baptism of changed hearts and lives for the forgiveness of sins.

Mark 1:4

Before Jesus started His ministry on earth, God sent a guy ahead of Him to let people know what, or rather Who, was coming. His name was John, and they called him John the Baptist because he spent most of his time baptizing people in the Jordan River. (*Baptizing* means dipping someone in water to show they're forgiven and washed clean of the bad stuff they've done.)

John the Baptist was related to Jesus; he was His cousin, which is kind of cool. John's main message was for the people to turn from their wicked ways, start following God, and get ready because God was about to visit the world in the person of Jesus.

John lived out in the wilderness near the river and wore a coat made of camel's hair. Matthew's description of John mentions that he wore a leather belt around his waist (Matt. 3:4). Is that important? Could be. Because in the Old Testament book of 2 Kings, Elijah, one of the greatest prophets in history, also wore a leather belt around his waist (2 Kings 1:8), so Matthew definitely wanted his readers to make the connection between John the Baptist and Elijah.

And did John really eat bugs? It sure looks that way. According to Mark 1:6, John ate honey and locusts (or grasshoppers)—yuck. I really wouldn't advise doing this at home. Some people think that the Scripture refers to a tree whose fruit is described as the locust bean, but most people think that John really did eat the bugs. Gross.

Jesus loved and respected John. Once He even told His disciples that John was the greatest person who ever lived.

Not everyone felt the same about John. At one point, he was arrested and executed because he confronted King Herod, the evil king of Israel.

But John was obedient to the Lord and did what God wanted Him to do. As a result, he was one of the first to recognize that Jesus was the One who was going to save the people from their sins (John 1:29).

Will there be video games in heaven? How about art or entertainment?

No one has ever seen this.
   No one has ever heard about it.
No one has ever imagined
   what God has prepared for those
   who love him.

1 Corinthians 2:9

As far as we know, we won't have video games, movies, or entertainment in heaven. I mean, if you think about it, when we're there we're going to be in the presence of the God who created the entire universe! He made the sun and all the billions of stars. He created and *knows* every single person who's ever lived. Most of us watch movies or play games to experience an exciting adventure, but life in heaven will be one amazing, awesome adventure. And it'll be real! That'll be so much more exciting than any movie or game could ever be. If you think of it that way, you realize we're not going to need any movies or entertainment at all.

There's nothing wrong with movies or video games (but remember to take a break from them once in a while!), but heaven is going to be so awesome, we probably won't even think about them. We'll be able to talk to God and share our lives with Him anytime we want! Not to mention all the cool people we'll get to know up there.

Here's a fun thing to think about, even though there's nothing in the Bible that says this: Wouldn't it be cool if, when we're in heaven, since we'll be outside of time up there, we'll be able to watch amazing historical events happen? Things like Noah's big flood. Or David defeating Goliath? Or Jesus walking on water? Or the Wright brothers flying their first plane? That would be pretty cool if it could happen.

As far as art and music are concerned, will they continue? It's hard to know for sure, but since God created all of us to create *with* Him, it seems He would want us to continue doing that for Him in heaven. *But wait!* you might say. *I'm not creative! I*

like math and science. Or, *I like to build things.* Or, *I'm really good at fixing things.* Are you kidding? That's creative! Creativity is not just used in the arts. You might be a creative baker or carpenter. You might be good at farming, repairing cars, or taking care of animals. God gave each of us creative gifts to use with Him and for Him, and chances are, He'll continue and maybe even expand our creativity when we get to heaven.

Will we get along with everyone in heaven? Even people we don't like?

Do your best to live in peace with everyone.

Romans 12:18

This is a great question! There's probably been someone in your life you didn't get along with or somebody you just didn't like. In fact, you might *still* not get along with them! But what happens if you run into them in heaven? Will you still have the same feelings? Will they? Well, the good news is, if you should happen to run into them up in heaven—and trust me, you will—you'll both be different. In fact, believe it or not, you'll both be perfect, and yes, you will get along.

Because the other person will be changed, and guess what? You will be too! And maybe you've been driving *them* crazy all this time!

The stuff that hurts friendships, like jealousy, gossip, envy, trash-talking, loneliness, and meanness, won't exist up in heaven, so whatever it was that came between you two will literally be a thing of the past.

But you don't have to wait for heaven to develop a good relationship with the person who's driving you crazy. Here are a few steps that might help you do it right now:

1. Try to forgive them. If they did something mean to you, ask God to help you forgive them. It might be hard, and it might take a little time, but begin to take steps to forgive them.

2. Pray for them. It's hard to dislike or be mad at someone you're praying for.

3. You might even try to think of one or two things that are good about the person and dwell on those. They might be good at music or maybe they like their dog or have a cool sweatshirt. Look for something that's good about them.

4. Who knows? Sometimes the people who drive us the craziest at first end up being our close friends after a while. Give them a chance.

PS: If somebody is bullying you or abusing you in any way, you need to stay away from them and tell someone about what's going on. This person is *not* your friend.

TALK IT OVER

Getting Along with Difficult People

Let's face it, life isn't perfect, and it seems like there will always be some people in our lives we have trouble getting along with.

1. Is there somebody in your life right now you're having trouble loving? (Don't mention them by name—just say yes or no.)
2. What's going on between you and the person?
3. Is there a possibility that *you* might be part of the problem?
4. In one of Paul's letters, he says that as far as you can, try and be at peace with everyone. What can you do in this situation to help work it out?

Spend a few minutes sharing prayer requests. If you're having problems with somebody, ask God to help you love that person.

Should I really forgive someone who's hurt me?

Be kind and loving to each other. Forgive each other just as God forgave you in Christ.

Ephesians 4:32

Has anyone ever hurt you? Maybe they pushed you or made fun of you. Maybe somebody left you out of their group or hurt your feelings. That doesn't feel very good, does it? And because it hurts way down deep inside, sometimes we get mad and want to treat those people the same way they treated us.

But . . .

God wants us to learn to forgive those people rather than try to get back at them.

Why?

Because God knows that if we carry hurt and unforgiveness for a long time, it starts to hurt *us. How can that be?* Well, God knows how we work; in fact, He knows us better than we even know ourselves. And He knows that if we hang on to anger and hurt, it starts to affect us in other ways. It makes us sad, fearful, irritated, or even lonely. So He wants us to forgive the people who have hurt us. Doing so is good for us.

Wow, sounds good, but how? How do I forgive someone who's been really mean to me? Good question.

First, when somebody hurts you or says something mean to you, it's okay to say, "That really hurts my feelings." Let them know you don't like what they're doing. If they're really a friend, they'll stop.

After somebody hurts you, it's okay to hurt for a little while; that's just human. Sometimes it'll take a long time until you get to where you even *want* to forgive the person, and that's okay too. If that's the case, you might ask God to help you begin to *want* to forgive them.

And guess what? He will!

Later, when you're thinking about what they did or said, ask God to help you forgive them. It might take some time and effort, but it'll be worth it. Then try praying for the person. After a while, you might get to a place where you can forgive them.

Were there really spies in the Bible? Who were they? Did they ever get caught?

Joshua son of Nun secretly sent out two spies from Acacia. Joshua said to them, "Go and look at the land. Look closely at the city of Jericho."

Joshua 2:1

Some people think reading the Bible isn't going to be any fun. But when you start getting into it, you'll discover the Bible is full of exciting stories. There are battles and miracles and kings and queens. There are brothers who are always fighting, seas that dry up so people can walk through, and even a talking donkey! And yes, there are a couple stories that include spies.

1. When God's people had come out of Egypt and were about to enter the promised land, Joshua decided to send two spies into the city of Jericho to check it out. They snuck into the city and hid at the house of a woman named Rahab. When

172

the soldiers came looking for them, Rahab hid the spies in a bunch of grain she happened to have up on her roof. She told the soldiers that the guys must have snuck out of town and that if they left that minute, they might be able to catch up to them. While it's never good to lie, she did help the two spies escape, and they went back and reported to Joshua what had happened. As a result of Rahab's help and her faith in God, she and her family were rescued when Joshua and the people attacked Jericho. Check it out in Joshua 2.

2. David used spies to report to him what King Saul was doing when Saul was trying to chase down and capture David. And later, when David became king, his son Absalom tried to take over the country. David asked a couple young men—Jonathan and Ahimaaz—to spy on Absalom so David would know what he was planning. The spies avoided going into the city because they might have been caught, so a servant girl helped relay secret messages to them. Later, they left and had to hide in a well. The lady of the house covered the mouth of the well with a sheet and spread—you guessed it—grain all over the sheet. So once again, God used a clever woman and a bunch of grain to protect His two spies. And

this time, God and His spies helped King David escape.

So you see, spies have been around for thousands of years, and often in the Bible they end up helping and protecting God's people.

Is hell a real place?

Enter through the narrow gate. The road that leads to
hell is a very easy road. And the gate to hell is very wide.
Matthew 7:13

This is a really important question. When you think
about hell, it can sound like a made-up place or a
fantasy. But just as heaven is a real place where followers
of God will be with Him forever, hell is a real place where
people will be separated from God forever.

Now think about that for a moment. To be separated
from God means to be separated from all His goodness.
There won't be any forests anymore. Or oceans. Or mountains. Or friends or music or art or anything beautiful. For
everything that's wonderful and beautiful and pleasing
and fun comes from God. So why would you ever want
to be separated from Him?

How do we know hell is a real place? Here are a couple
reasons:

1. The Bible talks about hell a lot. And we can believe the Bible because it's God's Word to us.

2. Jesus talked about hell. And He didn't talk about it like it was just a state of mind or a dream. He told His followers that hell was a place of darkness and even punishment. Yikes!

That sounds bad! Who would want to be separated from God and His love and healing? But God loves us so much that He opened the doors of heaven through His Son, Jesus. So now not one single person ever has to spend forever separated from God. We'll talk about how God and Jesus opened up heaven for us a little later.

What's hell like?

Those people will be punished with a destruction that continues forever. They will not be allowed to be with the Lord, and they will be kept away from his great power.

2 Thessalonians 1:9

Talking about hell might be interesting, but the main thing you want to know about hell is that you don't ever want to go there!

Hell is a place with no connection to God at all. There won't be any of the beauty, love, care, peace, or joy we know even now here on earth. None of the great things God's created will be there because He won't be there either.

We get most of our information about hell from Jesus Himself. He talks about it several times in the New Testament.

1. Jesus describes hell as a place of darkness. Have you ever been somewhere, maybe a basement or out in the forest camping, and it was so dark you

couldn't even see your hand in front of your face? Hell's kind of like that, only worse. You get the idea.

2. He also describes hell as a place of punishment. People will be punished for the bad things they've done in this life.

3. It'll be a place of loneliness. Whew. That doesn't sound like much fun. So if you ever hear people joke about wanting to go to hell because that's where their friends will be, that's the wrong idea. It'll be a place of extreme loneliness.

4. Apparently, God didn't create hell for people at all. It was created as a place of punishment for the devil and the angels who follow him.

Why would God send anyone to hell?

These people will go off to be punished forever. But the good people will go to live forever.

Matthew 25:46

As we talked about in the last two questions, hell is not a place you ever want to go. It's a place of darkness and loneliness and a place without any connection to God at all. So why would God send people there?

People have been asking this question for centuries, and it's a good one. I mean, after all, if God's supposed to love all of us, why would He send somebody away from His love, kindness, and goodness?

Well, the truth is, God doesn't ever send anybody to hell. He's done everything He can to make sure nobody in the world ever has to even get near it. We all deserve to go to hell because we've all done stuff that has hurt ourselves and other people. We've either said or done something that wasn't right or good and ended up harming someone.

But there was only one person in history who never did, said, or even THOUGHT anything bad, and that was Jesus. And God's good plan was to let Jesus take our place, die, and be separated from God so that we never have to.

And that's good news! So why do some people go to hell? Think of it this way: Let's say there's been a big flood in your town, and the whole place—houses, stores, schools, parks, and playgrounds—have all been covered by ten feet of water. There's a guy on the roof of his house, and somebody comes by with a boat and offers to help him. But the guy on the roof says, "No thanks, I don't think this will be too bad. I can do it on my own. Besides I don't like your boat that much. Thanks, but go help somebody else." Whose fault would it be that the guy never got off the roof? The guy in the boat or the guy on the roof? The boat owner did everything he could to save the guy on the roof, but it was up to the guy on the roof to decide to get in the boat.

So just like the guy with the boat, God has done everything He can do to give us a way to escape hell and punishment. It's up to us to say yes and get in God's boat.

Can God help me make good decisions?

Trust the Lord with all your heart.
    Don't depend on your own understanding.
Remember the Lord in everything you do.
    And he will give you success.

Proverbs 3:5–6

Life is full of choices, and God wants you to make great choices that will help you, your family, and your friends. But making good decisions is hard sometimes. Especially when you're only a kid!

Here are five steps to help you make good decisions:

Step 1: Read God's Word—Is what you're about to do okay with the Bible? If you're tempted to cheat on a test or during a game, it's probably not a good decision. Are you thinking of being mean to someone or picking on them? The Bible would probably say no. Are you thinking of helping the kid next door or helping your mom or dad with

181

something? The Bible would say that sounds like a good decision!

Step 2: Pray—God wants us to involve Him in every decision we make. Ask Him if what you're planning is a good idea. He might not speak out loud to you, but sometimes you'll get a feeling or thought that will help you know if this is what God wants for you or not.

Step 3: Get some advice—If you're trying to do the right thing in a situation and you're not sure the best way to go, ask for some advice. Find an older person who loves God and ask them what they think you should do. You might talk to your mom or dad or a teacher, pastor, or coach to get some good advice. After all, they're older and they might have been through just what you're going through. Learn from these people.

Step 4: Pay attention to your feelings—If you really want to do something (and you know it's not wrong; see above), then you should check out your own desires. If you have a certain talent or skill, like sports, music, art, or helping people, that might be one way God's showing you what you should do. If you love working with animals, maybe volunteering at a shelter could be fun for you. If you're a good listener, God might use you to help people who are going through a hard time. One of the fun things about growing up is discovering who God made you to be!

Step 5: Watch how things work out—This seems pretty simple, but one way God helps direct us is by how things work (or don't work) out. For example, you might think it would be cool to skip from, say, the third grade to high school. But as you've probably figured out, that may not happen. You might really want a puppy, and after a while your mom and dad start to soften a little bit, then pretty soon you've got a dog sharing your bed! Sometimes God uses our circumstances to show us the best things He has for our lives.

If you need to make an important decision, try following these steps. They should help when you're trying to figure out the best way to go.

Will I still be myself in heaven? Will I still have my same personality?

I praise you because you made me in an amazing
and wonderful way.

Psalm 139:14

Some people think that when we get to heaven, we'll be really different than we are now. Maybe more serious or grown-up. Or who knows? Maybe everyone will be exactly alike.

Sounds kind of boring.

But think about it—who's the most creative person in the entire universe? God, of course! He created each and every one of us with our different hair color, freckles, eye color, and laugh. Before you were even born, He knew how tall you were going to be, what your favorite color would be, and what kind of ice cream you'd like.

So it seems like if God is that creative, then He must have given you the personality you have right now. You're special and one of a kind!

So chances are, you're going to bring that amazing personality of yours right into heaven with you. Your humor, your intelligence, the way you look at things, and the way you talk. You'll really be *you* there!

The cool thing, though, is that you'll be the BEST YOU EVER!

You'll be yourself, all right, but you're going to be your perfect self, with no insecurities, fears, hurts, or worries!

Will we be all serious in heaven or will we have fun?

And the streets will be filled with boys and girls playing.

Zechariah 8:5

If you're like most people, you think your life is pretty good. You get to play, work sometimes, sleep, hang out with friends, and eat good food. You get to joke around and even enjoy good music. So since this life is pretty fun and interesting, you might think that heaven will be boring and serious.

But actually, heaven's going to be the most exciting, fun, and amazing place you could ever imagine. While we're not exactly sure what we'll be doing up there, we do know that God is going to be there, and wherever He is, it's always amazing and awesome.

And there will be laughter, music, friends, family, and a close friendship with the God who created you and knows everything about you. And as we mentioned in question 68, you're going to be *you* with no limits!

So everything about heaven is going to be perfect, including you and everything you do!

What are some of your favorite things to do? Play sports? Sing? Draw pictures? Play with your dog or cat? Do you think we'll be doing those things in heaven?

Doesn't everybody go to heaven?

Peter said to them, "Change your hearts and lives and be baptized, each one of you, in the name of Jesus Christ for the forgiveness of your sins. And you will receive the gift of the Holy Spirit."

Acts 2:38

Even though God loves everybody and wants to live with them forever, the truth is that not everyone will go to heaven when they die. Jesus was clear that the people who decide to follow Him during this life will get to be with Him in heaven.

Since heaven is the place where God lives, and because some people want to have nothing to do with Him in this life, chances are they won't choose to be with Him in heaven.

God is a perfect God who can't be in relationship with sin or the bad stuff we do, and since we all do bad stuff, we're separated from Him.

But the good news is that God loves us so much, He took care of the sin problem for us. Since sin, or bad stuff, keeps us separated from God, Jesus came and took that punishment for us!

When Jesus hung on the cross, He was separated from God the Father for the first time in eternity. And His perfect sacrifice paid the price so that we (or anyone who decides to) can go to heaven when we die. Check out page 265 to see how to start a friendship with God through Jesus.

DID YOU KNOW?

There is an entire book in the Bible that never mentions God. Not even once! It's the book of Esther in the Old Testament, the story of a young Jewish girl who ends up helping save the entire Jewish population. And even though God isn't mentioned, it's pretty evident that He's involved behind the scenes in bringing about the miraculous protection of His people. Check it out in the book of Esther.

Who was Daniel? Did he really spend the night with a bunch of lions?

He said, "Daniel, servant of the living God! Has your God that you always worship been able to save you from the lions?"

Daniel 6:20

Daniel was a young guy in the Old Testament (in fact, he even has his own book there) who had a really interesting life. He was probably a teenager when his hometown of Jerusalem was surrounded and attacked by this huge army from Babylon. Daniel and a bunch of his friends were taken captive and moved to Babylon, where the king—Nebuchadnezzar—chose a bunch of these young people to be trained to become his advisors.

Daniel and three of his friends were chosen to help the king out. But even though they lived in Babylon, a godless empire, they didn't give in to the culture around them. They continued to love and serve God, and for the most part, things worked out for them. The king loved them and trusted their judgment above his other advisors'.

But then one day when a new king, Darius, came along, some of the other leaders of the country got jealous of Daniel and tried to figure out a way to destroy him. Since he never seemed to do anything wrong and was loyal to the king, they decided to make a law that Daniel would be forced to break. They made it illegal to pray to anybody but the king. Well, there was no way Daniel was going to pray to a person, so he continued in his prayer life, praying to the one true God.

When the bad guys reported Daniel to the king, the king was in a tough spot. He loved Daniel, but he knew he had to enforce the law. They brought Daniel before the king, and he was sentenced to be eaten by lions. Ew.

They took Daniel and threw him into the lions' den, and you'll never guess what happened! God kept the lions from attacking or even bothering Daniel. It must have been some kind of night. Daniel was in there with some hungry lions, and yet they ignored him all night long.

When the sun came up, the king ran to the lions' den and called out to Daniel. "Daniel, did your God whom you serve protect you from the lions?"

And Daniel shouted back, "Yes, He protected me all night long."

So Daniel was shielded from the lions, and his enemies were defeated. God proved to Daniel that He would take care of him and protect him. Even in a lions' den!

Why does it make me anxious to think about dying and going to heaven?

There the people who sat in darkness have seen a great Light; they sat in the land of death, and the Light broke through upon them.

Matthew 4:16 TLB

Because we've never died before, dying is a mysterious thing, so it's natural to be anxious about it. In fact, there were even people in the Bible who were afraid of dying.

Remember the disciples when they were caught in a big storm in the middle of the Sea of Galilee? Check it out in Luke 4. They came to Jesus and said, "Teacher, do you care about us? We will drown!"

And a good king in the Old Testament named Hezekiah heard that he was going to die soon, and he wept. The good news for him was that God heard his prayer and gave Him many more years to live.

But why are we afraid of dying? Think of it this way: If you could remember things from when you were in your mom's tummy, you might have thought, *Gee, it's nice in here. I can sleep whenever I want, Mom's feeding me whenever I want to eat, and it's pretty cozy, safe, and warm.*

Then came the time for you to be born, and you might have thought, *Hold on a second—I don't want to do that! I don't know what to expect! I like it in here where I'm comfortable!* But then, of course, you were born, and your life really got exciting!

Just because you don't know everything that's to come doesn't mean you have to fear it. God's taking care of you and always will. Besides, if you follow Jesus, heaven is going to be so much more amazing than this life ever could be.

So it's okay to be a little anxious about dying, but the Bible says that Jesus can even take away our fear of death. Check out Hebrews 2:15: "Jesus became like men and died so that he could free them. They were like slaves all their lives because of their fear of death."

Just ask Jesus to help you with the things you're afraid of and He'll do it!

Talk It Over: Don't Be Afraid

Did you know that the phrase "Don't be afraid" (or "Fear not") appears in the Bible more than three hundred times? God knows that some things scare us, and yet He wants us to know that He's ALWAYS with us, protecting us and watching over us. He knows your name and He's holding on to you real tight as you go through all of life together.

1. When you were younger, what were some of the things that scared you? Do they still scare you?
2. Are there things in your life right now that scare you? What are some of them?
3. Why do you think it's not easy, and even scary, to talk about dying?
4. Does knowing that God is always with you and watching over you help you not to be so afraid of things?

What are some things you can pray about with your family? Do you have friends who might be anxious about things in their lives? Pray for them as well as for your own needs today.

Why doesn't God just use Zoom?

The Lord spoke to Moses face to face as a man speaks with his friend.

Exodus 33:11

Good idea! I mean, we've talked about how God is really different from us. He's a Spirit, so He doesn't have a body, and He's ginormous. In fact, He even created the whole universe! He's so powerful and He can do anything, so why not just appear to us, maybe on Zoom, and let us know what He's like? Make it easy. Show us how He feels about us, what He likes and doesn't like, and if He has feelings and emotions. Let us know if He laughs or cries and if He loves the same things we love. Come on, God, help us get to know You.

Wait a minute! He *did* do that. Not on Zoom but in *person*.

God became a person just like us, you know. He became a man—Jesus—so we could see exactly what God is like. For example, by looking at Jesus, we realize that God

- loves kids (Matt. 19:14)
- is powerful enough to control the weather (Matt. 8:23–27)
- has a sense of humor (Matt. 7:3–4; Luke 18:24–25)
- cares about lost people (Matt. 9:36)
- reaches out to people no one else cares about (Matt. 8:1–4)
- has compassion and even cries over hard things (John 11:34–36)

So yeah, God does all that for us, and He doesn't even need ZOOM!

Is God really watching me all the time? How does He do that?

Keep me as the apple of your eye;
hide me in the shadow of your wings.

Psalm 17:8 NIV

Yes, the truth is, God has promised not just to be watching you all the time but also to be with you wherever you go. Whether you're at school, at home, at the store, playing with friends, on your sports team, or at the lake, God promises always to be with you. You know why? Because He loves to be with you.

Think about one of your favorite friends. Or an uncle. Or a grandma. Isn't it nice to be with them? You laugh together, share memories, and just have fun.

That's how God feels about you.

As for *how* He does it, that's a great question. With almost eight billion people on earth right now, how does God have time to see and notice everybody? It's mind-boggling!

Maybe this will help—God lives in heaven in an eternal state (which is just a fancy way of saying He lives *outside* of time, remember?). So while we're limited by time (and space, now that we think about it), God isn't. In fact, He created time, so He's not limited by it. And since He's outside of time, He can be anywhere and everywhere at once! Don't ask how it works, but it does.

So somehow God can be with each one of us all the time, hear our prayers, and even help us get to know Him every single day.

Our part is to open up to God and continue to get to know Him too.

God's with You All the Time

Believe it or not, God is big enough and amazing enough to know what's going on with every one of us all the time. He knows when you're excited about your new kitten, He knows when you've hit a home run at recess, and He knows when you're feeling lonely or left out because you didn't get invited to someone's birthday party.

1. Is there someone in your life who always makes you feel good when you're around them? Who is it? What do you like about them?

2. If you could tell God one thing, what would it be?

3. How does it make you feel when you hear that God is watching you all the time? Does it give you comfort or make you nervous? Why?

4. Is it hard for you to understand that God can watch over every single person in the world at one time?

How will our friendship with God be different in heaven from how it is on earth?

A servant does not know what his master is doing. But now I call you friends because I have made known to you everything I heard from my Father.

John 15:15

You might have been following Jesus all your life, or your friendship with Him might be brand-new. But one thing is for sure—your friendship with God is based on faith right now. In other words, you love Him, you trust Him, you believe in Him, you even talk to Him, but you've never seen Him!

Jesus thought that was cool. In John 20:29, while He was speaking to His disciples, He said, "You believe because you see me. Those who believe without seeing me will be truly happy." He knew that all of us who would follow Him without ever meeting Him in person would be happy. Because faith and believing are important to God.

But when we get to heaven, things will be different. Instead of believing something or someone we can't see, we'll actually see Jesus and God the Father face-to-face and in person. And anytime we want! After all, you're one of God's kids.

Heaven is going to be so much better than life here on earth because we'll be with Jesus all the time. So yes, your friendship with God will be different in heaven because you'll see Him and talk to Him just like a friend. That's pretty awesome!

76

If God forgives me when I do something wrong, can I just keep doing bad stuff?

I will forgive them for the wicked things they did.
I will not remember their sins anymore.

Jeremiah 31:34

It's such great news to know for certain that when we do something wrong, God is always willing to forgive us. In fact, the Bible tells us that not only does God forgive us when we're truly sorry and ask Him to but He also chooses to *forget* the bad stuff we do too. So does that mean we can go on doing bad stuff to ourselves and other people? No, not at all.

God knows that the bad stuff we do isn't good for us, and He loves us so much that He doesn't want anything to ever hurt us.

Besides, when we love someone, a mom, a dad, a friend, or a brother or sister, we don't want to keep doing things that hurt them. The same goes for our friendship with God. We want to please Him in everything we do.

So how do we stop doing these things we don't want to do? When you do or say something that hurts another person (and who doesn't?), try these steps:

1. Tell God you're sorry and ask Him to forgive you. And He will!

2. Do you need to apologize to someone for what you did? That might be important too.

3. If you're having trouble in some area of your life—lying, hitting, being mean, or picking on someone—and you can't control yourself, ask God to help you. He wants you to be free from this even more than you do!

77

Did the walls of Jericho really fall down when the people shouted?

When the priests blew the trumpets, the people shouted. At the sound of the trumpets and the people's shout, the walls fell.

Joshua 6:20

There's a great account in the Old Testament book of Joshua in which God has an interesting battle plan to attack the evil city of Jericho. Jericho is one of the oldest cities in the world, and at the time, it was surrounded by a tall wall. I mean, we're talking like fifteen feet high! Attacking it would seem impossible. But God had a plan. And it seemed really strange. He told Joshua to have all the people walk around the outside of the wall once a day for six days. Then on the seventh day, they were to walk around it seven times. Then they were to stop and shout at the top of their lungs (don't try this at home) and God would do the rest.

The people obeyed. They marched around the walls for six days, then on the seventh day, they marched again, stopped, and shouted.

And guess what? The walls fell down flat, and God's people ran in and took the city. What an amazing story! But did it really happen?

For a long time, people doubted the story—it *is* a strange one, after all. It sounds almost made up. But in the last hundred years, archaeologists have found evidence that, yes, Jericho's walls did indeed fall down flat at one point. They've found rubble and bricks that seem to prove that the walls fell down all at once one day in the city's history.

So it looks like this amazing story really did happen. After all, God is pretty big and powerful. Knocking over a big, fat wall wouldn't be too much trouble for Him. You can read the whole story in Joshua 6.

78

Will we laugh in heaven?

A happy heart is like good medicine.

Proverbs 17:22

Some people—maybe even you—think that heaven is going to be really serious all the time. But what if it's not?

Remember, God created our sense of humor and laughter. He's the one who gave laughter to the human race, so it seems unlikely that He wouldn't want us to laugh and have fun in heaven.

Have you ever laughed so hard you were almost crying? Maybe it was with a good friend, your mom or dad, or maybe one of your siblings.

Part of the fun in that is the relationship you have with the other person. And since God is all about relationships, I think He'll enjoy us having a good time and even laughing with each other up in heaven.

We won't use any mean or cutting humor, and no one will make fun of anyone else, but I really believe we'll be laughing in heaven.

What are some things that make you laugh? Your dad? Funny movies? A certain friend?

Does God really hear all our prayers? How does He do that?

Then you will call my name. You will come to me and pray to me. And I will listen to you.

Jeremiah 29:12

With all the people on earth and so many of them praying or talking to God, how in the world does He hear, much less answer, everybody's prayers? It seems impossible! But we need to remember that God isn't just a bigger, stronger, more amazing version of a man. He's the One who came up with and created everything in our whole universe.

Plus, as I mentioned before, God lives in eternity. That means He lives *outside* of time. He's not limited to being in one place—or one time—like we all are. So somehow He can be completely with us whenever we need Him. He can hear us, understand us, and care about us in ways that nobody else can. Pretty cool, huh?

God loves it when we talk to Him. Really! He loves when we include Him in everything we do—school, play, sports, our families, everything!

Praying is just talking to God like a friend. What are some things you'd like to tell God right now?

Your Direct Line to God

God loves it when we pray. Sometimes people pray in church with formal-sounding, serious prayers, while other times, people just talk to God as if they're walking down the street with their best friend. There's no real right way to pray. Just remember that God is always listening.

1. Do you have a best friend? Do you talk to them all the time or just on Sunday? God is just like your friend; He wants you to talk to Him all the time.

2. Why do you think God wants you to pray?

3. When you pray, are you supposed to say certain words, or can you just talk to God like He's a friend?

4. God loves it when we invite Him into what we're doing, whether it's the good stuff or the hard stuff. Why do you suppose that is?

What are some things you'd like to pray about right now? Do you need His help with something? Or do you want to thank Him for something He's already done for you? Go ahead and tell Him. (If you don't feel like praying out loud, that's okay. God can still hear us, even when we're praying silently.)

Did Jesus really say that only kids can go to heaven? Why did He say that?

I tell you the truth. You must accept God's kingdom like a little child, or you will never enter it!

Luke 18:17

Back in Jesus's time, kids weren't thought of as very important. When boys turned twelve years old, they were taken a little more seriously because they were beginning to understand more about God and their role in the family. But before that, they weren't treated as special.

There's a story in the Bible that's a favorite of mine. It's found in Luke 18:15–17.

One day some moms brought their little kids to Jesus so He could bless them. But some of Jesus's friends, the disciples, tried to shoo them away. (Has this ever happened to you?) Maybe they thought Jesus was way too important and busy to bother with a bunch of little kids.

Well, Jesus wasn't very happy with the disciples' actions. He said, "Don't keep the children away from Me!

Theirs is the kingdom of heaven. In fact, if you don't become like a little child, you won't enter the kingdom at all!" This was pretty shocking for Jesus's disciples to hear, as well as for the other people standing there listening to Him.

But Jesus wasn't saying that only kids could go to heaven. He meant that all of us—old and young alike—need to come to Him like a child. Think about what that means. Children are happy, trusting, loving, and innocent. So what Jesus was saying was that we need to come to Him just like that, trusting, loving, and believing. And then we can have a friendship with Him that will lead us to abundant life here and now and forever with Him in heaven. So people of any age can start a friendship with Jesus no matter how old—or young—they are!

Why do people think of angels wearing robes, playing harps, and sitting on clouds when they think of heaven?

> I will praise you with a harp,
> God, my God.
>
> Psalm 43:4

If you ever see cartoons or even some books about heaven, you might see drawings of people sitting on clouds in robes, strumming harps. Where did we get that picture of heaven anyway?

There are lots of times harps are mentioned in the Bible. Most of the time, they're mentioned in the Psalms and in other parts throughout the Old Testament.

But in the last book of the Bible, Revelation, there are mentions of people in heaven worshiping God, and some are even playing harps. Revelation 5:8 says, "After he took the scroll, the four living things and the 24 elders bowed down before the Lamb. Each one of them had a harp." (No one is completely sure who the twenty-four elders are, but they might represent the twelve tribes of Israel in the Old Testament and Jesus's twelve disciples in the New Testament. This shows how the Old Testament and the New Testament come together in Jesus.)

And why clouds? I guess this idea comes from the fact that we know that heaven is somehow above us. After Jesus was resurrected, He went up into the sky until a cloud covered Him. That might be where that idea came from. When we think of the sky, we often think of clouds. But as I mentioned in question 1, heaven won't be misty or invisible at all. It's a real, solid place that's even more real than the world we live in now. Hard to understand, but it's true.

And as far as where the white robes idea came from, it's probably Isaiah 61:10, which says, "Let me tell you how happy God has made me! For he has clothed me with garments of salvation and draped about me the robe of righteousness" (TLB), and Revelation 6:11, which says, "Then each one of these souls was given a white robe. They were told to wait a short time longer."

People saw these verses and assumed we'd be wearing white robes and playing harps. And you know what? We will be clothed in white because we'll be forgiven and cleansed of all our sin. And apparently some people will be playing harps up there.

Some people say they've talked to dead people. Is that okay?

Some people say, "Ask the mediums and fortune-tellers what to do. They whisper and mutter and ask dead people what to do." But I tell you that people should ask their God for help.

Isaiah 8:19

Since all of us have been made in God's image and even know that there is something more than just this life, it's natural to want to explore things of the spirit, things we can't see or hear. Ecclesiastes 3:11 says, "[God] has made everything beautiful in its time. Also, He has put eternity in their hearts, except that no one can find out the work that God does from beginning to end" (NKJV).

Unfortunately, some people think they can go to a fortune teller or have some kind of séance in order to speak to someone who's already died. You might have even seen TV shows or movies where people talk to the dead, but that's not what God wants for us. The Scripture above—Isaiah 8:19—says we should avoid seeking to speak to the dead. If we need wisdom, we should ask God.

God strictly warns all of us against trying to contact a dead person. It might be tempting to have your fortune told or to play with a Ouija board or even to check out your horoscope, but God wants us to always look to Him alone for wisdom regarding our lives and our futures.

He even promises that if we need to know something, we can come to Him and He will give us all we need to know. James 1:5 says, "But if any of you needs wisdom, you should ask God for it. God is generous. He enjoys giving to all people, so God will give you wisdom."

So if you're ever tempted to try to contact someone who already died, remember these two things:

1. It's impossible. You can't speak to anybody who already died.
2. God forbids us from even trying; He knows that doing so isn't good for us and can open us up to some confusing and even scary things.

The best thing to do is go to God. He'll help you do the right thing. He might not tell you the future, but He promises to be with you as you move forward.

Will there be pizza in heaven?

The Lord of heaven's armies will give a feast.
It will be on this mountain for all people.

Isaiah 25:6

It's hard to imagine heaven without pizza, ice cream, candy, and cupcakes, isn't it?

I mean, there's something really fun and yummy about enjoying some tasty food, especially when you're with friends and family members. And what can be better than sharing a nice, hot pizza covered with pepperoni, cheese, sausage, and pineapple? Or maybe no pineapple.

Even though nobody's sure what kind of food there's going to be in heaven, whatever it is, it's going to be amazing! And from what it sounds like, you'll be able to eat all you want. Think about it; it's God's all-you-can-eat banquet!

Jesus told stories about the heavenly banquet on more than one occasion. In Luke 14, He shares that the banquet (or heaven) will be open to anyone who wants to come. But they need to answer His invitation to start a friendship with God through Him.

With all those people coming, we'll need one long banquet table!

And you'll be sitting at the table (or tables?) with such cool people as Paul, Peter, John the Baptist, King David, Solomon, Samson, Queen Esther, and Jesus's mother, Mary. You might even get to introduce one of these great people to pepperoni pizza, Snickers, or a Big Mac. And the best thing is that God the Father and Jesus will be at the table too.

Pass the napkins!

How long is eternity?

From eternity to eternity I am God. No one can oppose what I do.

Isaiah 43:13 TLB

Since we live in a world of time and space, eternity is something we really have a hard time understanding. I mean, it's like . . . always! And once we get to heaven, we'll live in perfect bodies that never get sick or tired, and we'll be that way forever!

But how long is eternity? It might be described like this:

Imagine a cable stretching from Los Angeles, California, on the West Coast all the way to New York City on the East Coast. If you can look at a map of the United States to see how far that is, it will be helpful. So picture a cable stretching all the way across the country.

Now let's say you have a felt marker, and you make a mark on the cable. Just a quick line somewhere along the way. Okay, get ready—that mark is like our life. And the cable represents eternity, or forever. Whoa. That cable goes a long way, and that mark isn't very big.

This is kind of a silly illustration, but it might give you an idea just how long eternity is. In fact, the only difference between our imaginary cable and eternity is that eternity doesn't stop at New York City. It keeps going on into infinity.

Whoa. I need to sit down for a minute.

DID YOU KNOW?

When Jesus was born in Bethlehem, how many wise men came to visit Him?

A. 3   C. 80
B. 120   D. Who knows?

Believe it or not, the answer is D, "Who knows?" The Bible never says how many wise men, or Magi, came to visit the baby Jesus. Most people figure it was three because they showed up with three gifts—gold, frankincense, and myrrh—but we don't know for sure.

By the way, gold was a gift fit for a king, frankincense was used in temple worship, so it showed that Jesus was worthy of worship, and myrrh was used when burying people. This showed that Jesus was going to die for our sins!

Wait a second. . .

Will there be cell phones in heaven?

On the day I called to you, you answered me.

Psalm 138:3

You might have a cell phone already, or maybe not, but they definitely seem to be everywhere! Some people are sure they couldn't live without their cell phone. But even though the Bible never mentions cell phones (or TV, movies, or laptops, for that matter), we can guess we won't have cell phones in heaven. But don't worry; we won't need them!

It seems like in heaven we'll be able to communicate and talk to one another anytime we want. And in person! How do we know that? Well, one way is by once again looking at Jesus after He died and came back to life on Easter morning.

Even though He was real and not a ghost, He apparently could appear and disappear whenever He wanted to (Luke 24:31). He also was able to come through locked doors without opening them (check out John 20:19)!

So if Jesus could be wherever he wanted whenever He wanted after He rose from the dead, it seems like we'll be able to do the same thing. Do you want to talk to your cousin? There you are! Or do you want to see your best

friend? You won't have to pick up your phone. They'll be right there in front of you!

There's nothing wrong with cell phones at all—in fact, they're really useful sometimes—but it seems like God likes us to meet face-to-face with Him and with one another!

Are there things I can do to make God smile?

May the Lord bless and protect you; may the Lord's face radiate with joy because of you; may he be gracious to you, show you his favor, and give you his peace.

Numbers 6:24–26 TLB

Did you know there are things you can do that make God happy? Things like being obedient to your parents and teachers, loving the people around you (even your siblings), and maybe helping a kid at school or someone in your neighborhood.

Talking to God makes Him smile as well. And realizing that you're His kid and that He loves you—this makes Him happy too.

What are five things you can do today that will make God smile?

Did Jesus really squish mud in somebody's face? Why did He do that?

After Jesus said this, he spit on the ground and made some mud with it. He put the mud on the man's eyes.

John 9:6

Wow! Did that really happen? What was going on that day? Well, don't get the wrong idea. Jesus didn't do it to make fun of or pick on the guy. Jesus did it for a very important reason.

One day Jesus and His friends the disciples were over by the big temple in Israel's capital city, Jerusalem. They saw a man who had been blind since he was born. He had never seen the sky, trees, birds, or even his mom or dad. The disciples figured either the man who was blind or his parents must have done something really bad to make God mad enough to make this guy blind. But Jesus said that wasn't true. He knew what He was going to do. And it was going to make God even more famous that day.

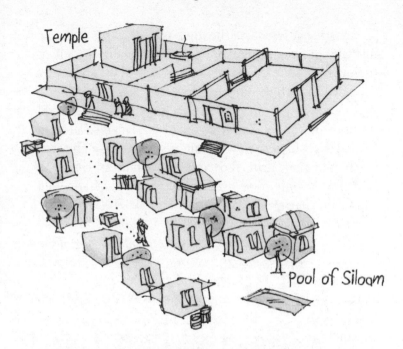

Temple

Pool of Siloam

So Jesus went over to the man and spit on the ground. *Really? Jesus did that?* Yup. It's right there in John 9:6. Jesus mixed the dirt around and made some mud, then He put it on the man's eyes. The guy must have been pretty surprised!

Then Jesus said, "Go and wash in the Pool of Siloam" (John 9:7). The man obeyed Jesus, walked through town, and washed in the pool. And guess what? The minute he washed, he could see! He was no longer blind!

So why did Jesus use the mud and send this guy on a walk for him to get healed? Jesus could have just spoken the word and the guy would have received his sight, just like He did with Bartimaeus in Mark 10:46–52.

Could it be that the guy in this story not only needed to be healed of his blindness but also needed to learn to trust Jesus? It took a lot of faith to walk through town with mud all over his face and go wash off in the pool. But the man did obey Jesus, and two things happened that day:

1. He was healed and could see!
2. He learned to trust Jesus and do what He said.

So even though Jesus did something that seems really weird to us today, it was important for the guy to learn to trust Jesus and obey Him.

Is Jesus really coming back again to take us to heaven? When?

No one knows when that day or time will be. The Son and the angels in heaven don't know. Only the Father knows.

Mark 13:32

When Jesus came to earth two thousand years ago, He came quietly. He was born in a small town in Israel called Bethlehem. Instead of being born in a palace, He spent His first night in a stable, and instead of being surrounded by servants and royalty, He was surrounded by donkeys, sheep, and maybe a cow or two. Most people slept through His arrival.

But the Bible tells us that He's coming again, and this time nobody will miss it. When He comes back the second time, He'll make all things right, and at some point He'll take all His followers who are still alive up to heaven with Him. (His followers who died before will already be in heaven.) Jesus will rule and reign in a new earth with His angels and us!

And from then on, there will be no more pain or tears or death.

So when is He coming back? That is a question that lots of people have been asking for a long time. Even the first followers of Jesus thought He'd come back during their lifetime. In fact, every generation since has been sure He'd come back while they were still alive. But when Jesus was here on earth, He told His disciples that even *He* didn't know when He'd be coming back. He said that only God the Father knows the time and date, so it is impossible to tell for sure when it will happen.

The important question for us isn't *when* Jesus is coming back but what we should be doing in the meantime. Here's a hint: We should get to know God through reading His Word, the Bible, through talking to Him by praying whenever we can, and through hanging out with other people who love God. It's also important to tell our friends about Jesus and how much He loves them. That way they and *you* will be ready whenever Jesus returns.

Did Jesus really bring someone back to life?

After Jesus said this, he added, "Our friend Lazarus has fallen asleep. But I am going there to wake him."

John 11:11

Since Jesus is God in human form, it seems like He can do anything He wants, so making a dead guy come back to life wouldn't be all that hard. But remember, back in Jesus's day, the people around Him had a hard time believing He really was God.

So anyway, this guy Jesus loved named Lazarus got sick. His sisters Mary and Martha sent word to Jesus to come and heal him, but Jesus stayed where He was for three more days. During that time, Lazarus died. When Jesus did finally come, they had already laid Lazarus in a tomb. Martha came to Jesus and said, "If you had been here, my brother would not have died" (John 11:21). Jesus told her that her brother would rise again, and Martha said, "I know that he will rise and live again in the resurrection on the last day" (John 11:24).

But Jesus was talking about right then and there. He went to the tomb, prayed to God the Father, and then called, "Lazarus, come out!" (John 11:43). And a couple seconds later, Lazarus came walking out of the tomb! Can you imagine how happy Lazarus's sisters were? Jesus had restored their brother to them.

You can read the entire story in John 11 in the New Testament.

Jesus also brought two other people back to life: a little girl (Mark 5:35–43) and a young man (Luke 7:11–17).

How did Jesus make it possible for me to go to heaven?

For God loved the world so much that he gave his only Son. God gave his Son so that whoever believes in him may not be lost, but have eternal life.

John 3:16

There are a lot of people who figure that if you're good enough—like if you do more good things than bad things—you'll go to heaven. But that's not what the Bible says. Romans 3:23 says, "All people have sinned and are not good enough for God's glory." Whoa. That means all of us.

We've all broken God's law and aren't good enough for God's glory. None of us will ever be good enough to work our way to heaven.

But there is *good* news. Jesus actually lived His whole life without ever doing anything wrong. He never even had a bad thought! He was the only one who was good enough to take the punishment we deserve so that we could go free. The innocent for the guilty.

When Jesus was thirty-three years old, His friends deserted Him, His enemies captured Him, and the Romans took Him and sentenced Him to death. They led Jesus out of Jerusalem up to a hill called Calvary and hung Him on a cross. He died in agony up there, but that wasn't the worst part. While Jesus hung there, God turned His back on Jesus, and their relationship was broken. For the first time in eternity, God the Father and God the Son were separated. Jesus went through that so we will never have to.

Jesus took our place—the perfect for the imperfect—and opened heaven up for all of us.

So what do we do? How do we receive Jesus's sacrifice for us and begin a friendship with Him? Check out page 265 to find out the ABCs of how to become a friend of Jesus.

Why did Jesus come here? Isn't heaven much cooler?

> Christ himself was like God in everything. . . .
> He gave up his place with God and made himself
>   nothing.
>   He was born as a man
>   and became like a servant.
>
> Philippians 2:6–7

Heaven for sure is way cooler than earth, but God has us here at this time, in our family, at our school, and in our neighborhood for good reasons. And Jesus left heaven and came here to earth for important reasons too. Here are the two most important ones:

1. Jesus came down from heaven to show us what God was like. Since God is GINORMOUS (He did create all the universes, after all) and since He is Spirit and we can't see Him, He's pretty hard to figure out. So by becoming a human and hanging out with us, Jesus was able to show us what God is like. When we look at Jesus, we realize that:

God is powerful.

He loves and cares for lonely and hurting people.

He doesn't want us to be afraid.

He knows us by name.

See what I mean? If we ever wonder what God is like, we just have to look at Jesus. But He came for another even more important reason.

2. Jesus came to open the way to heaven for us. Since God is perfect and we're not—we do bad stuff—there's no way we could live with God forever in heaven. We'd spoil it! But God didn't want to live without us. He couldn't just ignore our bad stuff; someone had to pay the penalty. So He sent Jesus not only to show us what God was like but to take the penalty for our sin. Like we saw in the last question, since Jesus lived a perfect life, He was the only one who could pay the price. So while Jesus was hanging on the cross, God left Him. Abandoned Him. Because of that, we never have to be separated from God. Ever.

And because Jesus obeyed the Father and took the punishment for us, He now lives in heaven and welcomes all of us who believe in Him to come live with Him forever. That's good news!

Did Jesus always heal everyone in the same way?

Jesus touched the man and said, "I want to heal you. Be healed!"

Matthew 8:3

This is a great question and something that's a bit of a mystery as we read the New Testament. Let's look at some of the different ways Jesus healed people:

1. **The guy who couldn't walk,** who was lowered down through a hole in a roof in front of Jesus. Jesus said, "Your sins are forgiven." Then He said, "Get up, take up your mat, and walk." The guy was healed, got up, and walked out. (See Luke 5:17–26.)

2. **Bartimaeus, who couldn't see.** Jesus asked him, "What do you want me to do for you?" Bartimaeus replied, "Teacher, I want to see again." Jesus said, "Go. You are healed because you believed." And just like that, Bartimaeus could see, and he followed Jesus on the road. (See Mark 10:46–52.)

3. **The man outside the temple who was born blind.** Jesus spit on the ground and made mud, squished it in the guy's face, then told him to walk through town to the Pool of Siloam and wash it off. The guy did what he was told and was healed. (See John 9:1–12.)

4. **Another guy who was blind** was brought by friends to Jesus for healing. Jesus took the man by the hand and led him outside the village. Then Jesus spit on the man's eyes and asked, "What do you see?" The man replied, "I see men walking but they look like trees." Jesus touched his eyes again and the man could see everything clearly. (See Mark 8:22–26.)

5. **The nobleman's son.** This is a great one. Jesus was in a town called Cana and a nobleman showed up. He'd traveled all the way from Capernaum to ask Jesus to heal his son who was sick. Capernaum was about sixteen miles away from Cana. Jesus said to him, "Go your way, your son lives." The man believed Jesus and the boy was healed. From sixteen miles away! (See John 4:46–54.)

6. **A woman who was bleeding.** Jesus was walking through a crowd on his way to heal a little girl when a woman reached out and touched the edge of His robe. This woman had had uncontrolled bleeding for twelve years. As soon as she touched

Jesus's garment, she was healed instantly! She didn't talk to Him before, and He didn't speak to her until after she was healed. (See Mark 5:25–34.)

7. **The ten lepers.** Jesus and His disciples were walking through a village in Samaria in northern Israel when ten guys with leprosy called out to Him. Leprosy was an awful disease that usually was a death sentence. When they called out to Jesus, He told them, "Go show yourselves to the priests." (Back then if someone was healed from leprosy, they needed to go to the priests to be checked out and declared clean.) So these guys obeyed Jesus and as they went, they were healed. By the way, only one of them came back to thank Jesus and praise God. (See Luke 17:11–19.)

As we read the New Testament, we realize that Jesus healed people in a whole bunch of different ways. Maybe He did this to show that He was God and always did things in a creative way. Also, Jesus knew exactly what each person needed, not only to be healed of their disease but also to begin a friendship with Him.

important stuff you need to know

What's another way I can make God smile?

Give thanks whatever happens. That is what God wants for you in Christ Jesus.

1 Thessalonians 5:18

Remember, God loves you no matter what! No matter what you do or who you are or where you live or who you hang out with, He loves you and that'll never change. But there are some things we can do that make God happy. Plus, making God happy is really good for us too, so that's a win-win!

One of the things that God loves is when we're thankful. Even when you're having a hard day—maybe your hair's sticking out all funny, your best friend had lunch with somebody else, and you still can't spell the word *between* on the test—you still have a lot to be thankful for. There's even a story in Luke 17:11–19 where Jesus heals ten guys with leprosy, but only one of them returns to thank Him for what He's done. That guy not only gets healed but ends up close to Jesus!

God loves when we're thankful to Him for all the good things He's given us. Think about it; your family probably has a house or an apartment. Your parents may have a car, a TV, and a cell phone. You probably have food and a place to sleep and friends and maybe even brothers and sisters.

So even on a hard day, you should be able to think of some things to be thankful for. When we're thankful, we're telling God that He's doing a really good job of taking care of us. It's like when someone gives you a gift. You always want to say thank you, don't you? When something happens that's really great, like scoring a goal in soccer, getting an A on a test, drawing a cool picture, or teaching your dog a new trick, take a second and say "Thanks, God." Because after all, He gave you the talent and skill to do those things.

It's okay to ask God for things, but always remember how much He's done for us already. In fact, one of the best things to be thankful for is that God created heaven just for you and all the people who love Him. That's a great thing to be thankful for!

List five things you can be thankful for right now.

94

Are there really gates in heaven? What about Saint Peter? Does he have the keys?

I will give you the keys of the kingdom of heaven.

Matthew 16:19

When Jesus asked His disciples who people thought He was, they told Him some thought He was John the Baptist and some thought He was Elijah from the Old Testament or one of the other prophets. But Peter said, "You are the Christ, the Son of the living God" (Matt. 16:16). Jesus told Peter he was right and that Peter was going to get the keys of the kingdom of heaven. Now a lot of people picture Peter up at the gates letting people in, but that's not what Jesus meant. He was telling Peter that the fact that He—Jesus—was indeed the Son of God was going to be the foundation of His church. The church would be built on that truth. And the "keys" Jesus gave Peter were the keys of authority that Peter—and all of us—can enjoy. For example, we can talk to God anytime, and we can even help our friends understand the love and forgiveness of God.

As far as if there are actual gates in heaven, the book of Revelation mentions gates as part of the new city—the New Jerusalem—that will appear after Jesus comes back.

> The city had a great high wall with 12 gates. There were 12 angels at the gates. On each gate was written the name of 1 of the 12 tribes of Israel. (Rev. 21:12)

So there will be twelve gates, three on each of the four sides of the city, and they'll be open all the time. Sometimes when we think of gates, we think that they're closed to keep people out. But the truth is, God's gates to heaven are always open to anyone who wants to begin a friendship with Him through Jesus.

important stuff you need to know

Why does bad stuff happen?

We know that in everything God works for the good of those who love him. They are the people God called, because that was his plan.

Romans 8:28

Sometimes when bad stuff happens in our lives, like if somebody treats us really mean, if we feel lonely or sad, or if our parents aren't getting along, it might be easy to think that God doesn't care or that He has forgotten about us. But even when you might feel that way, that's not the truth. God never forgets us and never abandons us. He loves us and always wants the best for us. So if that's true, why does bad stuff happen?

When God created the world way back when, things were perfect. Nobody died or even got sick. People loved one another and even got to talk to God like He was a friend. But when Adam and Eve disobeyed God, things got bad really fast.

Suddenly people started fighting one another, people got sick, and death, disease, and injuries came into the world. Even nature got messed up: Hurricanes, floods, and tornadoes started happening, and volcanoes started erupting. So you see, the whole world got affected. And ever since then, bad stuff has happened all over the world.

Another thing to remember is that God gives us the freedom to choose to do whatever we want, just like He gave Adam and Eve. And because of that, people can even end up hurting one another.

But the good news is, when God allows something hard to come into our lives, He always has a plan to turn it around for good. Sometimes it's the hard things that make us call out to God and get closer to Him.

Remember, God never *causes* the bad things in our lives, but sometimes He allows them so He can make them into something good.

And there are probably hundreds of times God protects us from bad stuff and we may never even know it.

Why Is This Happening?

If God is perfect and He loves us, why do hard things like loneliness, anger, and hurt feelings happen? Why do we get sick or sad or not get along with someone? These are great questions.

1. If you were God, would you let bad things happen? What would you do differently?

2. Why do you suppose God allows hard stuff into our lives and our world?

3. Can you think of a time that was really hard for you? Tell about what happened.

4. Have you ever done something that hurt yourself or somebody else? What happened?

5. What do you suppose God would like us to do when bad things happen to or around us?

Go ahead and ask God to help you with a hard thing you're going through. If things are going great, tell Him "Thank You"!

What should I do when hard things happen in my life?

The Lord is good.
> He gives protection in times of trouble.
> He knows who trusts in him.

Nahum 1:7

As I mentioned in the last question, when bad stuff starts to happen to us or around us, we might feel like God's forgotten all about us. So what are some things we can do when hard stuff starts happening?

1. **Tell God about it.** And be honest. If you're feeling sad or lonely or even mad, let God know. He wants you to tell Him everything that's going on in your heart. That's what praying is all about. You can even tell Him you feel like He's left you. Then ask Him to help you. He loves you and really wants good things for you.

2. **Believe** that God can use what's going on for good. Just like in the story of Joseph and his brothers, God can turn bad stuff around and make it good. Trust that He has a plan for you and that it's going to be great.

3. **Find a Friend.** If things seem really hard and you're not getting any better, it's good to talk to another person about it. It might be your mom or dad, an older friend, a pastor, or a teacher. Make sure it's someone who loves God and loves you. They might have good advice for you, and together you can figure out the best thing to do.

Write God a note telling Him what's going on in your life. Be honest and let Him know how you're feeling, good or bad.

Why doesn't the Old Testament mention Jesus?

You carefully study the Scriptures because you think that they give you eternal life. Those are the same Scriptures that tell about me [Jesus]!

John 5:39

When you first take a look at your Bible, it might seem like two different books. The Old Testament is all about battles and bad guys, prophets and kings. And the New Testament is all about Jesus. But believe it or not, get ready—the Old Testament is all about Jesus too!

Even though He's never mentioned by name, Jesus is throughout the entire Old Testament.

From the third chapter of Genesis through the book of Joshua and into the last book of the Old Testament, God refers to Jesus—the coming Savior.

Here are just a few examples:

1. A guy named Isaiah wrote about Jesus in the ninth chapter of his book. Isaiah lived over six hundred years before Jesus!

> A child will be born to us.
>> God will give a son to us.
>> He will be responsible for leading the people.
> His name will be Wonderful Counselor, Powerful God,
>> Father Who Lives Forever, Prince of Peace. (Isa. 9:6)

That sure sounds like Jesus!

2. In the Old Testament book of Micah, chapter 5, Micah says,

> But you, Bethlehem Ephrathah,
>> are one of the smallest towns in Judah.
> But from you will come one who will rule Israel
>> for me. (v. 2)

Bethlehem is the town where Jesus was born.

3. Psalm 22 talks about Jesus on the cross:

> My God, my God, why have you left me alone? . . .
>> Men make fun of me.
>> They look down on me.
> Everyone who looks at me laughs.

> They stick out their tongues.
> They shake their heads.
> They say, "Turn to the Lord for help.
>   Maybe he will save you.
> If he likes you,
>   maybe he will rescue you." (vv. 1, 6–8)

4. Psalm 16:10 talks about Jesus's resurrection hundreds of years before it happens!

> This is because you will not leave me in the grave.
>   You will not let your holy one rot.

A lot of the stories in the Old Testament point to Jesus in small ways: Jonah spending three days inside the fish is like Jesus spending three days inside the tomb after He was crucified. Abraham almost sacrificing his son and God supplying a ram to take the boy's place is a picture of how Jesus took our place when He died for our sins.

So you see, Jesus is all throughout the Old Testament. God was helping His people get ready for His arrival.

As you read through the Old Testament, what other verses sound like they're talking about Jesus?

What are five words you won't hear in heaven?

Therefore encourage one another with these words.

1 Thessalonians 4:18 NIV

Did you know there are some words we'll never hear once we're in heaven with Jesus? Here are just a few:

Frighten. You won't hear that word in heaven because you'll never be scared, frightened, or anxious ever again.

Ouch! You won't ever need to say that word again because in heaven there won't be any pain or anything that hurts us.

Allergy. Are you allergic to something? Grass? Pollen? Pets? The good news is, you won't be allergic in heaven! (Did you know that some cats are allergic to people?)

Tired. "I'm so tired." Have you ever said that or felt that way? In heaven we'll never feel tired. We'll have endless energy!

Goodbye. In heaven there are no goodbyes because our family and friends who love Jesus will be there with us forever! How cool is that?

Phrases we won't hear in heaven either:

Be careful! Since we won't ever get hurt or be in any danger in heaven, we won't ever have to say this to each other.

Sorry I'm late. Since we'll be living outside of time in heaven, we won't ever have to worry about being, well . . . on time.

I'm so lonely. You'll never be lonely in heaven because you'll have lots of people in your life who are now your brothers and sisters. Besides, Jesus is always going to be with you.

DID YOU KNOW?

Did you know there are several kids in the Bible who did some amazing things? You already know about David defeating the giant Goliath, but there are a few more kids who did some cool things:

Samuel was just a young boy when he learned to listen to God. He became one of Israel's most important leaders.

Josiah became king of all Judah when he was just eight years old!

Mephibosheth was King Saul's grandson and Jonathan's child. When Jonathan died in battle, David took Mephibosheth into the palace and treated him like a son. Later, when David's son tried to take over the kingdom, Mephibosheth stayed loyal to his friend David.

Timothy came to love God as a little boy. After he grew up, he helped Paul pastor several churches all over the region.

Jesus was only twelve years old when He amazed the religious leaders with His wisdom and questions.

So you see, God can use every one of us, no matter how young we are!

Samuel   Josiah   Mephibosheth   Timothy   Jesus

Was Jesus really God in human form?

The Father and I are one.

John 10:30

Okay, this whole thing sounds a little, well, unbelievable. God decides to become a man and come down to earth to meet us and let us know what He's like. Wow! But think about it: God is so GINORMOUS and powerful, and by the way, *invisible*, becoming a man was the very best way to give us a glimpse of what He's really like. So in other words, whenever we look at Jesus, we know what God is like. But was Jesus *really* God in human form?

Let's look at a couple reasons we can believe Jesus really was God in human form:

1. Jesus said He was. In John 10:30, He says, "The Father and I are one." (By the way, He said this to a group of people who were ready to kill Him if He wasn't telling the truth.) And in John 14:9,

Jesus says, "He who has seen me has seen the Father." And the guys who wrote the New Testament believed Jesus was God. In fact, most of them were executed because they wouldn't deny that Jesus was the Son of God.

2. The many miracles Jesus performed while He was here on earth are also proof that He was who He said He was. Jesus did a lot of pretty amazing stuff. Things like healing people, walking on water, feeding five thousand people with a few fish and some bread, calming a storm, and even raising people from the dead! One of the reasons Jesus did miracles was to help people understand that He wasn't just a good teacher but God Himself.

So that leaves us with a couple choices: Either Jesus *believed* He was God but wasn't, which would mean He was confused. Or He *knew* He wasn't God but lied to people to fool them, which would mean He was deceitful. We know that's not true. Our third choice is, of course, that Jesus was who He said He was: the Creator of the entire universe in human form—God in the flesh.

Did Jesus really feed five thousand people with a kid's lunch? How did He do that?

The followers answered, "But we have only five loaves of bread and two fish." Jesus said, "Bring the bread and the fish to me."

Matthew 14:17–18

One day Jesus was out on a hillside talking to a huge group of people about God and how to follow Him. It was a beautiful spot, a grassy hillside overlooking the Sea of Galilee. It would have been the perfect spot for a picnic, except for one thing: Nobody had any food! That is, except one little boy whose mom had thought ahead and packed him a nice little lunch of five loaves of bread and two fish.

When it started to get late, Jesus's disciples came to Him and told Him to send everyone home so they could get something to eat.

Jesus told them, "You give them something to eat."

The disciples must have thought Jesus was joking. "Are you kidding? There are thousands of people here; it would take a year's salary to give them just a little bit of food!"

Jesus said, "What do you have?" They told Him about the little boy and his lunch but then said, "But that's just a little, certainly not enough to feed all these people."

Jesus had the disciples make everyone sit on the grass. Then He thanked God for the food and started handing it out to the disciples, who then passed it out to the people. Somehow as they continued coming back to Jesus, He had more food for them to hand out. By the time He was through, all the people—more than five thousand of them—had eaten and were satisfied. There were even

twelve baskets of leftovers, one for every one of Jesus's twelve disciples!

And all because of one little boy's generous gift of his lunch!

You can read this story in Matthew 14:13–21, Mark 6:30–44, Luke 9:10–17, and John 6:1–14.

In the story, Jesus asked His disciples, "What do you have?" They didn't have a lot, but what they did have they brought to Jesus.

What do *you* have? You might feel like that little boy on the hillside that day, like you don't have much to give away. But did you know that God has given you gifts, talents, and time that He might want you to give away to someone else? Are you good at basketball? You might teach a younger kid some of the tricks and skills you've learned. Are you a good artist? You might draw or paint a picture for a friend, grandparent, or parent. Are you really good at school? Not everyone is, so maybe you could help a kid in your class with their homework. There are so many ways to serve God by using what you have to serve people!

List some things you're really good at. How might you use those talents to serve God?

Isn't God too big to care about me?

> But why is man important to you?
>   Why do you take care of human beings?
> You made man a little lower than the angels.
>   And you crowned him with glory and honor.
>
> Psalm 8:4–5

We've spent a lot of time talking about how big God is—after all, He created the sun, the moon, every single star we can see, and all the ones we can't. He spoke and the Pacific Ocean, Rocky Mountains, Vermont, and Argentina were created. He made air, molecules, and even time! So how does someone who's so GINORMOUS have time to care about my problems? A lot of people—including adults—figure God's way too busy to care about them.

That's one of the most amazing things about God. Not only is He big enough to take care of your problems but He's also close enough to you to know every single thing going on in your life.

Okay, get ready to have your brain explode again! Jesus said in Matthew 10:30 that God even knows how many hairs are on your head. Whoa! God's paying attention!

Somehow God knows when you're happy, like when you've just made a new friend, or nervous, like when you're about to take a test or try out for a team, or feeling lonely, sad, excited, or mad.

Even though it's practically impossible to understand how God can know everything about all of us, we just need to believe He does. So what do we do about it?

Let God know how you're feeling and what you're going through. That's praying! You can tell Him everything about what's going on in your life and even ask Him to help you. And He will!

How do I become a Christian?

Becoming a Christian is simply deciding to follow Jesus, getting to know Him, and becoming best friends with Him. Even though it seems a little hard sometimes—mainly because you can't *see* Jesus—beginning a friendship with Him is as easy as ABC.

Admit that you do bad stuff and that there's no way you can ever be good enough to go to heaven.

Believe that Jesus is who He said He is—God's Son, who lived a perfect life and then went to the cross, died, and was separated from the Father so we never have to be. Also believe that Jesus beat death by rising from the dead to live forever.

Confess that Jesus isn't just your best friend but the King, the Ruler, the Boss of your life, and follow Him wherever He leads you.

Daily Bible Reading Plan

Here's a simple, easy Bible reading plan for you to try. It goes for thirty days and covers the first seven chapters of the Gospel of Mark in the New Testament (although it skips over some verses that are a little hard to understand).

Try reading for five minutes a day. Start by asking God to speak through His Word to you every time you read. If you miss a day, no worries! Just pick up the next day where you left off. And at the end of thirty days, why not keep going?

The Gospel of Mark

☐ **DAY 1: Read Mark 1:1–8**
John the Baptist

☐ **DAY 2: Read Mark 1:9–11**
John Baptizes Jesus

☐ **DAY 3: Read Mark 1:12–13**
Jesus Is Tempted in the Desert

☐ **DAY 4: Read Mark 1:14–15**
Jesus Begins to Teach

☐ **DAY 5: Read Mark 1:16–20**
Jesus Calls Four Fishermen to Follow Him

☐ **DAY 6: Read Mark 1:21–28**
Jesus Casts Out an Evil Spirit

☐ **DAY 7: Read Mark 1:29–34**
Jesus Heals Peter's Wife's Mother and a Lot of Others

☐ **DAY 8: Read Mark 1:35–39**
Jesus Prays and Teaches throughout Galilee

☐ **DAY 9: Read Mark 1:40–45**
Jesus Heals a Man with Leprosy

☐ **DAY 10: Read Mark 2:1–12**
Through the Roof!

☐ **DAY 11: Read Mark 2:13–17**
Jesus Calls a Tax Collector to Follow Him

☐ **DAY 12: Read Mark 3:1–6**
Jesus Heals on the Day of Rest

☐ **DAY 13: Read Mark 3:7–12**
People from All Over Come to Jesus

☐ **DAY 14: Read Mark 3:13–19**
Jesus Calls His Twelve Disciples

☐ **DAY 15: Read Mark 3:31–35**
Jesus's Mom and Brothers Come to See Him

☐ **DAY 16: Read Mark 4:1–9**
Jesus Tells a Parable about Planting Seeds

☐ **DAY 17: Read Mark 4:10–20**
Jesus Explains the Parable

☐ **DAY 18: Read Mark 4:21–25**
Listen and Learn from Jesus

☐ **DAY 19: Read Mark 4:30–34**
A Mustard Seed!

☐ **DAY 20: Read Mark 4:35–41**
Jesus Calms the Storm

☐ **DAY 21: Read Mark 5:1–20**
Jesus Casts Out Another Evil Spirit

☐ **DAY 22: Read Mark 5:21–24**
A Ruler Comes to Jesus for Help

☐ **DAY 23: Read Mark 5:25–34**
Jesus Heals a Woman and Hears Her Whole Story

☐ **DAY 24: Read Mark 5:35–43**
Jesus Heals the Ruler's Little Girl

☐ **DAY 25: Read Mark 6:1–6**
Jesus Is Rejected in His Hometown

☐ **DAY 26: Read Mark 6:7–13**
Jesus Sends Out His Disciples to Preach

☐ **DAY 27: Read Mark 6:30–44**
Feeding Five Thousand People!

☐ **DAY 28: Read Mark 6:45–52**
Jesus Walks on Water

☐ **DAY 29: Read Mark 6:53–56**
People Come to Jesus for Healing

☐ **DAY 30: Read Mark 7:24–30**
Jesus Heals a Woman's Daughter

Sandy Silverthorne has been writing and illustrating books for over twenty-five years, with nearly one million copies sold. He is the award-winning creator of the Great Bible Adventure children's series, several joke books for kids, *The Best Worst Dad Jokes*, and *Kids' Big Questions for God*. Sandy has worked as a cartoonist, author, illustrator, actor, pastor, speaker, and comedian. Apparently, it's hard for him to focus.

Connect with Sandy:

SandySilverthorneBooks.com

SandySilverthornesPage

Sandy Silverthorne